NEIL

BY JOHNNY ROGAN

Copyright © 1996 Johnny Rogan
Published by Omnibus Press (A Division of Book Sales Limited)

Edited by Chris Charlesworth
Cover & Book designed by 4i
Picture research by Johnny Rogan & Nikki Russell

ISBN 0.7119.5399.6 Order No.OP47807

Exclusive Distributors
Book Sales Limited, 8/9 Frith Street, London W1V 5TZ, UK.
Music Sales Corporation, 257 Park Avenue South, New York, NY 10010, USA.
Music Sales Pty Limited, 120 Rothschild Avenue, Rosebery, NSW 2018, Australia.

To the Music Trade only
Music Sales Limited, 8/9, Frith Street, London W1V 5TZ, UK.

Photo credits
All pictures supplied by LFI, Pictorial Press and Rex Features.

Every effort has been made to trace the copyright holders of the photographs in this book but one or two were unreachable. We would be grateful if the photographers concerned would contact us.

Printed in the United Kingdom by Ebenezer Baylis & Son, Worcester.

A catalogue record for this book is available from the British Library.

OMNIBUS PRESS
LONDON · NEW YORK · SYDNEY

CONTENTS

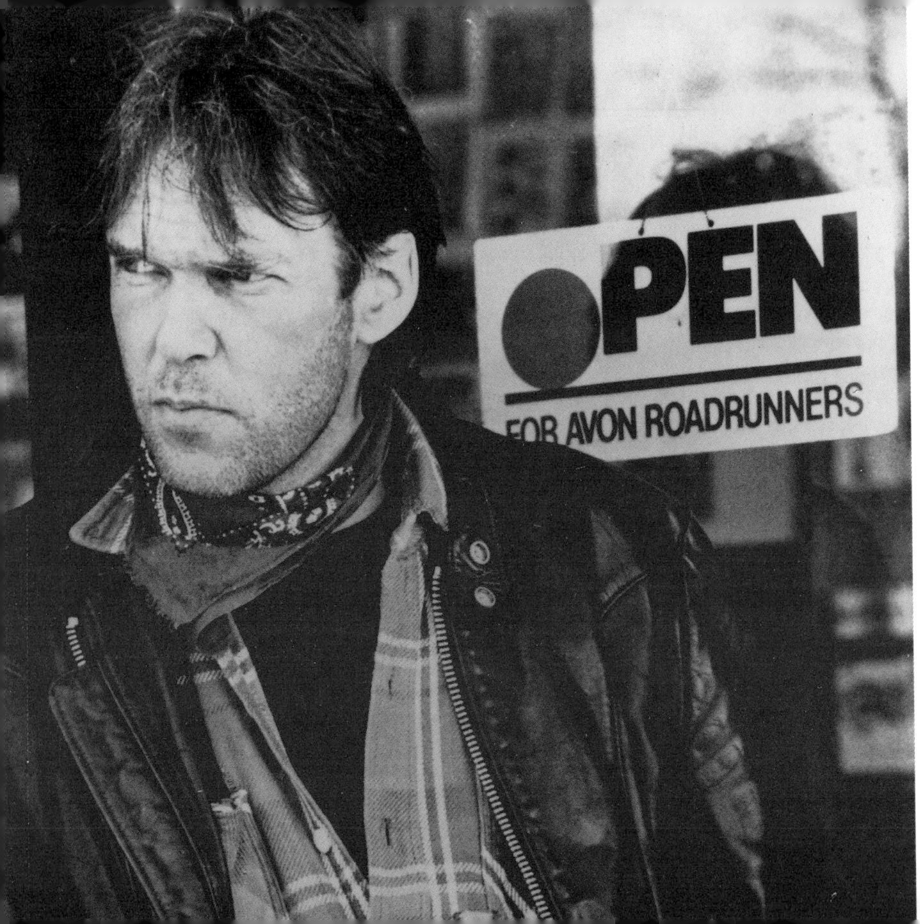
OPEN
FOR AVON ROADRUNNERS

INTRODUCTION

T here's a lot of information and critical analysis to fit into this tightly packed CD book, so I won't waste words on a lengthy introduction. Suffice to say, this book is concerned with Young's musical career on album from 'Buffalo Springfield' to 'Mirror Ball'. The emphasis here is on songs, not biography. I wrote this appraisal straight after researching *Crosby, Stills, Nash & Young: The Visual Documentary*, having also written a book on Young many years ago. It was a great pleasure to listen to all this material back to back and I hope some of you will be tempted to dig out these recordings and hear again the eclectic works of one of the most celebrated rock artistes of his generation. Release dates refer to the original US vinyl release; CD catalogue numbers have been omitted as Young's *complete* works have yet to be released in this format.

Any correspondence, flattering or abusive, is as welcome as ever.

JOHNNY ROGAN

STEREO SD 33-200-A

Buffalo Springfield

BUFFALO SPRINGFIELD

ORIGINAL RELEASE DATE: JANUARY 1967

The formation of Buffalo Springfield in the spring of 1966 saw Young team up with Stephen Stills, Richie Furay, Bruce Palmer and Dewey Martin in one of the most accomplished but self-destructive groups of the era. They achieved immediate fame in Hollywood where their live shows at the Whisky A-Go-Go were renowned for the dramatic guitar duels between Stills and Young. Widely tipped as the group most likely to follow The Byrds to international fame, they reputedly peaked as a live act during the first six to eight months of their career.

Their impressive début album featured seven songs composed by Stills and five by Young, with Furay completely missing out on any publishing income. Initial pressings of this record included Stills' 'Baby Don't Scold Me' but these were soon replaced by versions featuring another Stills' composition – the hit single 'For What It's Worth'. Despite Stephen's apparent ascendancy it was clear from the album that Young was, at least on this occasion, writing the more interesting material. Looking back at the work Stills conceded: "Neil's lyrics were superior to mine. His songs were like poems in a way, while I usually got straight to the point."

Below are the Young compositions featured on the album, although he would appear as lead vocalist on only two of them.

NOWADAYS CLANCY CAN'T EVEN SING

Prior to the release of their first album, this track was issued as a pilot single. Originally a B-side, it was promoted to A-side at the eleventh hour following favourable reports from distributors and radio stations. While achieving local hit status, its chances of breaking nationally were undermined by its length, lack of a memorable hook and the fact that it included the controversial word "damn" in the lyrics. With all these minuses to contend with, it was hardly surprising that the group and their record company were reluctant to allow Young's untrained vocal to feature on the recording. Instead, Richie Furay took the lead. Although he performed a competent job, much of the emotional fragility of Young's reading was lost in translation. Lyrically, the song is still intriguing, taking the form of a series of rhetorical questions which end in the surprise revelation that the mystery narrator is actually the songwriter himself.

FLYING ON THE GROUND IS WRONG

Richie Furay again takes lead vocal with Stills prominent in the backing and Young conspicuous by his absence. The song was the first of Young's speculations on the personal desolation that can accompany the onset of fame. On one level, the lyrics are typical of the period, using vaguely drug-related imagery to convey the emotional shock caused by a departing lover. However, Young then turns inward to reflect on the forces that have altered him ("...since I have changed/I can't take nothing home"). During the penultimate stanza he sets up an analogy between his own broken relationship and the bright city-like lights of a

country fair which dazzle rather than illuminate. As Young realises, the brighter the star shines, the greater is the glare on those with whom he wishes to become emotionally involved ("If I'm bright enough to see you/You're just too dark to care").

BURNED

This sounds like a premeditated attempt to rock up an average song in order to compensate for Young's vocal shortcomings. It was in fact his début as a lead singer in the Springfield and you can get the impression he rushed through the recording. As he recalled: "My first vocal ever done in a studio, late 1966 (Gold Star). The boys gave me some uppers to get my nerve up. Maybe you can hear that. I was living in a $12.50 per week apartment at the time and everybody on the floor liked it too. We stayed up all night listening to it."

DO I HAVE TO COME RIGHT OUT AND SAY IT?

Furay again takes lead vocal, a luxury which he regarded as a concession for losing out on the songwriting income. As he argued: "I think they had me sing a couple of Neil's songs just to appease me, to keep me satisfied because I had all the songs that made it on to the second album written when we recorded the first one." It's difficult to fault Furay's mannered performance here. He enunciates the lyrics perfectly and hits notes with a precision far beyond Young's capabilities. The song is strong too, detailing, in diffident terms, the problems of beginning a new relationship. Unfortunately, Young chose never to revive the song during his solo years, even though it would have been an appropriate choice for his acoustic set.

OUT OF MY MIND

Probably the highlight of the album, this was one of Young's most impressive songs of the period. An affecting guitar introduction is followed by Young's unusually precise diction, backed by sumptuous harmonies. Lyrically, the composition ably articulates his ambivalent feelings about fame and its attendant pressures ("All I hear are screams from outside the limousines/That are taking me out of my mind"). In many ways the song anticipates Young's insecurity about working within a group framework, a dilemma that would cause him to leave Buffalo Springfield on more than one occasion.

Full track listing: Baby Don't Scold Me (replaced by For What It's Worth); Go And Say Goodbye; Sit Down I Think I Love You; Nowadays Clancy Can't Even Sing; Hot Dusty Roads; Everybody's Wrong; Flying On The Ground Is Wrong; Burned; Do I Have To Come Right Out And Say It?; Leave; Out Of My Mind; Pay The Price.

BUFFALO SPRINGFIELD AGAIN

ORIGINAL RELEASE DATE: DECEMBER 1967

A year of turbulence preceded the release of this album, with Young leaving the group prior to an important television appearance on *The Tonight Show* and missing out on the Monterey Festival. Along the way, a proposed second album, *Stampede*, failed to reach completion and the group seemed likely to break up. However, by late summer 1967, Young returned, having worked with arranger Jack Nitzsche. His new direction was immediately evident on 'Buffalo Springfield Again' which is generally regarded as the group's finest album. It was a much more accomplished work than its predecessor with Stills emerging as an equal to Young by providing two of the famous songs in the group's repertoire: 'Rock & Roll Woman' and 'Bluebird'. Even Furay competed effectively with the charming 'A Child's Claim To Fame'. The new democracy evident on this album meant that only the following three Young compositions were included, but at least on this occasion he sang his own songs.

MR SOUL

Here, Young blatantly plagiarises the melody of The Rolling Stones' '(I Can't Get No) Satisfaction' and fuses it with a lyric more appropriate to '19th Nervous Breakdown'. The theme reiterates the mental turmoil of 'Out Of My Mind', although this time Young brings some humour to the proceedings ("Why in crowds just a trace of my face could seem so pleasing"). Dedicated to "the ladies of the Whisky A-Go-Go and the women of Hollywood", the song explores Young's ambivalent attitude towards stardom ("I was raised by the praise of a fan who said I upset her"). In portraying himself as "the clown" who does the "trick of disaster" he laments pop star fame, even though it is just beginning for the group. Interestingly, this song endured in Young's live set and was performed in radically different ways on both 'Trans' and 'Unplugged'. An alternate take of 'Mr Soul' can also be found on a 1971 reissued single.

EXPECTING TO FLY

This was actually recorded by Young during his estrangement from Buffalo Springfield in the summer of 1967. He had intended to pursue some solo work using Jack Nitzsche as arranger and this was one of the results. As he explained: "It took a lot of time. I overdubbed my vocal line by line to get it in pitch. Studio singing was still very nervous for me then. Though I was hot with the Springfield at the time. I brought the tape to record when we finally got together." When Young elected to rejoin the Springfield this was obviously a strong candidate for their album. The orchestral score by Nitzsche is enchanting, recalling his work with Phil Spector. Young's voice is quiet to the point of frail which adds an ethereal quality to the recording. Although Young would continue working with Nitzsche during the recording of his first solo album, the team would never produce anything quite as ambi-

tious as this again. It was an experiment which Young regrettably chose never to repeat.

BROKEN ARROW

The closing track on the album was Young's most ambitious work to date. He claims it took almost 100 takes to complete and at least two parts of the song are belatedly listed in the Atlantic archives under the titles 'Ball Park' and 'Theme Jazz'. Essentially, 'Broken Arrow' was a fascinating collage broken up into three separate sections in which Young discusses stardom, adolescence and idealised romance. Appropriately, the song opens with a snatch of 'Mr Soul' accompanied by the screaming of teenage fans. In fact, the first verse reiterates the theme of 'Mr Soul', analysing the symbiotic relationship between star and fan. The 'Ball Park' sounds introduce verse two in which Young deals with the generation gap, centring on a confused adolescent, repressed by maternal protection ("His mother had told him a trip was a fall/And don't mention babies at all"). Rolling drums and what sounds like a circus leads into the final section in which Young presents a fairy tale romance shrouded in allegory. The chorus returns for a final time, portraying an Indian holding a broken arrow, the symbol of peace. As Young acknowledged: "A broken arrow usually means that somebody has lost a lot". The track concludes with 'Theme Jazz', an uncredited borrowing featuring clarinet and piano, the latter possibly provided by Don Randi. Overall, this was an intriguing coda to the Springfield's most celebrated album.

Full track listing: Mr Soul; A Child's Claim To Fame; Everydays; Expecting To Fly; Bluebird; Hung Upside Down; Sad Memory; Good Time Boy; Rock & Roll Woman; Broken Arrow.

LAST TIME AROUND

ORIGINAL RELEASE DATE: AUGUST 1968

Buffalo Springfield's final album was a posthumous release compiled by Richie Furay and producer Jim Messina. The group had predictably broken-up, the victim of internal bickering, compounded by the on-off membership of Young and bassist Bruce Palmer. As Young explained: "I just couldn't handle it towards the end. My nerves couldn't handle the trip. It wasn't me scheming for a solo career, it wasn't anything but my nerves. I was going crazy, joining and quitting and joining again... I needed more space."

'Last Time Around' was, not surprisingly, an uneven album, with Furay at last in a position to ensure that his contributions were well represented. Young and Stills, by contrast, had already washed their hands of the Springfield and, for once, did not dispute the songwriting credits. Overall, the work was still fairly impressive, balancing Stills' Latin excursions with Furay's country rock and completely unexpected acid-tinged 'In The Hour Of Not Quite Rain'. Young's work was poorly represented in the final credits, with only two compositions and a collaboration to his name.

ON THE WAY HOME

Furay resumes lead vocal on this rather poppy reading of Young's look back on the history of the group ("Now I won't be back till later on/If I do come back at all"). There's even a string section in the middle for added commerciality. Significantly, the composition was later revived by Young as the opening number to his acoustic concerts and can also be heard on Crosby, Stills, Nash & Young's '4 Way Street'. The song serves equally well as Springfield pop and reflective singer-songwriter material.

IT'S SO HARD TO WAIT

Although credited to Furay/Young, the latter's involvement does not appear to extend much further than contributing some lines prior to the recording. It's a reasonable song but precious little to do with Young who was probably pleased enough to receive a co-credit.

I AM A CHILD

Technically, this hardly seemed a Springfield song at all, more an example of Young the soloist. As he explained: "The group was falling apart by this time. We cooked separately in the studios. The Sunset Sound receptionist's boyfriend on bass. The rest is me." The song, which some critics saw as a reply to Richie Furay's chiding 'A Child's Claim To Fame' on 'Buffalo Springfield Again', was more a personal view of Young's own loss of innocence. Here, he relates the innocence of infant curiosity and the greedy need for parental love ("I gave to you now you give to me"). The song had a surprisingly long life in Young's repertoire and was later used to theatrical effect in the film *Rust Never Sleeps* and the attendant 'Live Rust'.

Full track listing: On The Way Home; It's So Hard To Wait; Pretty Girl Why; Four Days Gone; Carefree Country Day; Special Care; The Hour Of Not Quite Rain; Questions; I Am A Child; Merry-Go-Round; Uno Mundo; Kind Woman.

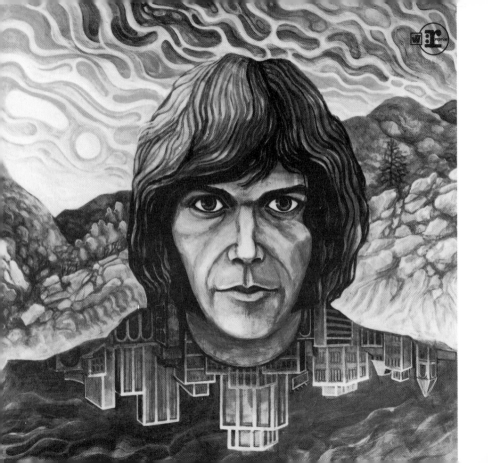

NEIL YOUNG

ORIGINAL RELEASE DATE: JANUARY 1969

While Stephen Stills remained with Atlantic Records, Young departed for a solo career with Frank Sinatra's label, Reprise. He also moved west to Topanga Canyon where he befriended producer David Briggs, who would work on the majority of his albums hereafter. For these sessions, however, Jack Nitzsche was still contributing some arranging and production ideas while Ry Cooder was also on hand with advice. Other players called upon during the late autumn of 1968 included bassist Jim Messina and drummer George Grantham, both on loan from the newly formed Poco. The resulting album was a highly impressive work, although it did not receive much press at the time and failed to dent the US Top 200 or achieve a UK release until much later in Young's career. He did the album no favours by constantly complaining about his vocals on the recording and forcing the company to finance a remix. According to Young the later remixed version transformed the album, but a close listen confirms that the differences were minimal. Some tracks sounded a little clearer and there was additional guitar work on 'Here We Are In The Years' and 'What Did You Do To My Life?' Beyond this though, there was precious little to choose between the original and later mixes and, for all his recommendations about the revised version, Young's vocal was still far from prominent. What Young's reasoning missed of course was the evident quality of the original recording. Although his vocal is buried deep at times, this actually enhances the mood of the album, as does the overdubbing which he later stated was not to his taste. In one sense, this album could be seen as the first of Young's genre experiments – an exercise in fusing folk and orchestral elements to great effect. There is no other work quite like this in the Young canon, mainly because he grew weary of the studio time involved in such a recording, preferring to record live and complete takes in a shorter period. It would be intriguing to see Young get back together with

Jack Nitzsche and attempt a work as disciplined as this again. It remains one of Young's most underrated works and I would be bold enough to place it among the best five albums he ever recorded.

THE EMPEROR OF WYOMING

Young opens his solo career with a jaunty instrumental as if defying the role of "singer songwriter" long before it is thrust upon him. It's interesting to note the country influence already present here and later to be developed more fully on *Harvest*.

THE LONER

The first song recorded for the album, with assistance from bassist Jim Messina and drummer George Grantham. It remains one of Young's best songs from the period, despite the low vocal mix. Lyrically, the sentiments shift from detached observation to a hint of sympathy in the final line ("On the day that she left he died but it did not show"). At the time, the identity of the loner was assumed to be Stephen Stills, but this was probably journalistic license. Ironically, Stills later recorded the song himself during the Seventies.

IF I COULD HAVE HER TONIGHT

A beautiful, understated melody is the highlight of this song of wish fulfilment. Young uses the unrequited love theme in several compositions on this album and this is a fine example of the tentative quality in his writing during this time. There is no known live performance of this in circulation, although it was probably played at some low key acoustic performances around the time of the album's release.

I'VE BEEN WAITING FOR YOU

A potentially powerhouse production complete with swirling organ is delicately held in check by the modest vocal mix. The track was recorded piecemeal, as Young explained in his familiar rambling fashion: "In the beginning we put down acoustic guitar and bass and drums, that's the smallest track I ever did, one guitar, bass and drums... Jimmy Messina, who plays the bass on it, played the bass part over and then he made up a different bass part so we took off the first one completely and played a whole new one... and then we dropped the acoustic guitar because it didn't fit with the other things that I put on... so then there was nothing left except for the drums. The pipe organ was put on...the vocal was done in a different studio... it does stick together though. It's very rare."

THE OLD LAUGHING LADY

Death is personified in the song's title as Young employs strings and a ghostly girl chorus to add to the eerie effects. Perhaps because an allegorical interpretation is inconclusive, the song retains its haunting appeal and mystery. Strangely enough, Young later revived this song in concert as an upbeat country number, completely at odds with its original execution. Later the song was chosen to open his 1993 *Unplugged* performance on MTV in an acoustic version that was played well but devoid of the mystery and sadness contained on the original.

STRING QUARTET FROM WHISKEY BOOT HILL

Producer/arranger Jack Nitzsche sets the scene for the second half of the album with this striking orchestral piece. 'Whiskey Boot Hill' would seem to be some grander concept that apparently remained unrealized, although

the title reappears as the centrepiece to the triptych 'Country Girl'.

HERE WE ARE IN THE YEARS

Undoubtedly one of the most seriously neglected songs in the Young canon, this telling ecological protest featured a striking arrangement, building to a steady and powerful conclusion. Regrettably, Young no longer features the song in performance, although its sentiments still sound contemporary, while its melody eclipses many of the weaker cuts in his current repertoire. Young admitted that he was attempting to make some sort of ecological comment without "going on a pollution and conservation kick".

WHAT DID YOU DO TO MY LIFE?

There is a delightfully child-like quality to Young's self-questioning here as he reflects on a fragmenting relationship. Indeed, some of the lines betray a tone of petulance ("I don't care if all of the mountains turn to dust in the air/It isn't fair..."), which is simultaneously amusing and poignant. The vocal mix ensures that each song segues unobtrusively into the next creating a sense of continuity and forming a coherent mood piece.

I'VE LOVED HER SO LONG

Another too often unheralded gem in the Young canon, this song mixes naturalistic and symbolic styles to striking effect in its depiction of the central female character. The whole is given even greater impact by the combined vocal forces of Merry Clayton, Brenda and Patricia Holloway, Gloria Richetta Jones, Sherlie Matthews and Gracie Nitzsche.

THE LAST TRIP TO TULSA

The lengthy closing track betrays Young's enduring debt to mid-period Bob Dylan. Here the surrealistic lyrics, complete with folk-rock style strumming guitar, take in the decline of religion, gender confusion, hippie paranoia and a series of vaguely autobiographical allusions ("I used to be a folk singer keeping managers alive"). In comparison to the other material on the album it sounds excessive and overtly self-conscious, but retains a period charm and remains a startlingly dramatic conclusion to an exceptional work. Immediately after the release of the album, Young insisted that this was a failed experiment but later revised his opinion sufficiently to feature an electric version of the song in live performance. Collectors can hear the latter on the B-side of the 1973 single 'Time Fades Away'.

EVERYBODY KNOWS
THIS IS NOWHERE

ORIGINAL RELEASE DATE: MAY 1969

The inspired teaming of Neil Young and Crazy Horse can be traced back to an appearance by The Rockets at the Whisky A-Go-Go in 1968. Young sat in with the group, which included Danny Whitten (guitar), Ralph Molina (drums) and Billy Talbot (bass). One year later, this nucleus of players would be recruited as Young's backing group and re-christened Crazy Horse. They would be fired, celebrated, abandoned and put on hold throughout Young's career, but whichever avenue he took, it seemed that he would always return to them. In a sense they represented the raw, emotional centre of his work. He frequently collaborated with infinitely superior musicians, but Crazy Horse were wonderfully empathetic feel players content to lock into a Young groove and bring out the emotive quality in his playing. They could rock hard, a feature that encouraged Young to describe them, clumsily but appropriately, as his own Rolling Stones.

This album achieved modest sales at the time of its release but it remains the definitive blueprint of the Crazy Horse sound. There's a touch of country rock here, some evocative ballads and even a frighteningly intense requiem that marries folk and contemporary rock. Despite these contrasting elements few would describe the work as eclectic. What lingers in the mind is the mesmerising guitar work, most notably on the tracks that close each half of the album. The songs themselves are simple but Young and Crazy Horse build them up layer by layer and through the use of repetition and refrain find a groove that is unique. Young could play with dozens of groups like Crazy Horse and attempt far more exciting guitar workouts, but there is a spirit here that somehow cannot be equalled. This is still Neil Young and Crazy Horse at their very best.

CINNAMON GIRL

An appropriate opening track inasmuch as it was the first song that they attempted together. One of the most durable numbers in Young's live set, this insistent rocker was particularly memorable for its engaging descending bass line and euphoric burst of lead guitar. The lyrics are exotic and allusive without really saying anything at all. As Young coyly noted: "Wrote this for a city girl on peeling pavement coming at me through Phil Ochs' eyes playing finger cymbals. It was hard to explain to my wife." The edited single version of the song, released in 1970, featured a couple of extra vocal exclamations.

EVERYBODY KNOWS THIS IS NOWHERE

An interesting, albeit slight, composition, with a leaning towards country rock. The strained harmonies are both attractive and whimsical, especially when compared to the more trained and disciplined work of Crosby, Stills & Nash. A radically different version of this song, minus Crazy Horse, can be heard on a rare US promo single.

ROUND AND ROUND

Although credited to Crazy Horse, this track actually featured Young, Danny Whitten and Robin Lane. The lyrics betray a passing debt to Kurt Vonnegut, but it is the haunting vocal work of Lane that makes the song so successful. Young was characteristically excited about the recording, although his comments degenerated into incoherence when recalling the session: "The echo from the acoustic guitar on the right echoes back on the left and the echo from the guitar on the left comes back on the right and it makes the guitars go like this... there's a one line start going like da-da-dnow... and then you can hear like one voice comes in and out and that's because Danny was rocking back and forth... those things are not featured, they're just in it..."

DOWN BY THE RIVER

The first of Young's guitar epics closes the opening half of the album. Building in intensity the song climaxes at each verse and Young implores "I shot my baby". It was an intriguing narrative that sounded as though it might have come from a newspaper report or local legend, but Young insisted that the words were

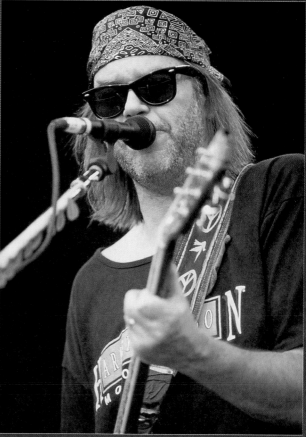

symbolic rather than literal. "Naw, there's no real murder in it," he claimed at the time. "It's about blowing your thing with a chick. See now in the beginning, it's 'I'll be on your side, you be on mine'. It could be anything. Then the chick thing comes in. Then at the end it's a whole other thing. It's a plea... a desperate cry."

A decade-and-a-half on, Young seemed more willing to accept that there was genuine violence at work in the composition. "Every once in a while you write a song and you do it many times," he remarked. "One night... you think, 'What's happening? I'm living this song!'" Young went on to claim that the song was about a disturbed man, who did actually shoot his lover: "He let the dark side come through a little too bright. One afternoon, he took a little stroll down through the field into the forest so that he could hear the water running along there. And he met this woman down there and he told her... he reached down into his pocket and pulled a little revolver out..."

The song became a *tour de force* when played by Crazy Horse and was later incorporated into CSN&Y's sets in 1969 where it was usually used as the final number. Later in Young's career the song was again

revamped for use by the International Harvesters. It remains one of the most enduring compositions to spring from Young's fevered imagination.

(WHEN YOU'RE ON) THE LOSING END

Ostensibly an upbeat country romp with a hoe-down conclusion, this song surprisingly contains some of the most pessimistic lyrics on the album and could equally have been performed as a melancholic lament. It would have fitted well into the repertoire of Young's International Harvesters but he resisted the temptation to revive it during his "country phase".

RUNNING DRY (REQUIEM FOR THE ROCKETS)

Arguably the most powerful track on the album, this revealed Young at his most compelling. Although the subtitle links the song with Crazy Horse's father group The Rockets, the lyrics are clearly concerned with the narrator's cruelty to a loved one. The *mea culpa* sentiments are given even greater force by the lachrymose violin work of Bobby Notkoff in what may be the most memorable guest appearance on any Young track. The confessional lyrics build to a climax of shame and regret only to be exorcised by passing time ("But soon these things are overcome and can't be recognised").

COWGIRL IN THE SAND

In common with 'Cinnamon Girl' and 'Down By The River' this was written while Young was recovering from a high fever. "Lying in bed sweating with scraps of paper covering the bed," as he put it. The oblique lyrics refer to an idealistic "woman of my dreams" who is herself idealised ("when so many love you, is it the same?"). Such lyrics are ultimately a mere backdrop to the extended instrumental breaks which arch steadily and inexorably towards the climactic three verses spread over 10 minutes. Over the years, this track has been rightly acclaimed as a prime example of Young's distinctive, brooding guitar work. At the time though, it did not bring him instant fame as a guitarist of merit. *Rolling Stone* reckoned his playing throughout this album was inferior to his work on its predecessor and, even in praising this song, it was the supposedly intense vocal performance that caught the critic's ear: "The lyrics are quietly accusative, while the lead guitar, alternatively soaring, piercing and driving, keeps the song surging forward. But it is Young's singing which is the real key to the success of this track. 'Cowgirl In The Sand' demonstrates quite clearly the peculiar depths of Young's voice. It indicates how rock manages, again and again, to triumph over high school music teachers and their legions."

Crosby, Stills, Nash & Young
Dallas Taylor & Greg Reeves

Déjà vu

DÉJÀ VU

ORIGINAL RELEASE DATE: MARCH 1970

Young's modest recording career took a decisive turn in 1969 when he was invited to join Crosby, Stills & Nash. They were already receiving premature plaudits as the most promising and accomplished ensemble of their era and their début album merely confirmed this world view. If ever the word "supergroup" meant anything, then CSN&Y were worthy recipients. Young brought a keener edge to their music and his electric interchanges with Stills were spectacular to behold. With 'Down By The River' providing a strong finale, Young's contribution to their live set was indisputable. He appeared with them at Woodstock, although he is not in the movie as he declined to be filmed while playing. On 'Woodstock II' you can hear the otherwise unavailable 'Sea Of Madness', a slight, organ-dominated track which is appealing rather than essential. While CS&N could have recruited a sideman of quality who was not a songwriter, they unselfishly allowed Young the chance to present his material to an audience that he might never have reached playing with Crazy Horse or singing solo.

This album looked like the start of a long and rewarding partnership but, frustratingly, it was to prove only one of two CSN&Y studio albums and its follow-up would not appear until as late as 1988. Much has been made of the fact that the foursome didn't appear together on every track but there was nothing unusual about that in rock music at the time. What is important is that the album had an aural unity, sounding like nothing else that had preceded it both in terms of production and performance. It was widely and wildly celebrated in the UK and established the foursome as kings of rock in the USA where it topped the charts. Young's influence on the album is strong, which is one of the reasons why you miss him so much on later CS&N releases. His searing guitar work alongside Stills on 'Woodstock' is still impressive and underrated. Even better is his contribution to Crosby's ultimate vision of

hippie paranoia 'Almost Cut My Hair'. Crosby and Young would work together again on the former's first solo album, and that was one combination that could have been used to far greater effect on several occasions over the past couple of decades. Apart from the above, Young also enjoyed the luxury of registering three writing credits on the album, as follows:

HELPLESS

Young's nostalgic vision of Omemee, Ontario has an unusually stoical tone as though it was written as a pastoral panacea to the problems of his present day life as an emerging rock star. CS&N provide a memorably strong harmonic blend with Crosby, as ever, adding depth to the melody.

COUNTRY GIRL

The power of Young's work with CS&N was seldom bettered than in this remarkable composition which was actually an amalgam of three song segments. Strongly influenced by Jack Nitzsche, it demonstrated Young's determination to emulate Phil Spector with a grandiose production. The results are magnificent with CS&N excelling themselves as the perfect back-up group. Regrettably, this represented the scale of Young's artistic ambition as a member of CSN&Y and he never again attempted an epic arrangement to match this singular achievement.

EVERYBODY I LOVE YOU

Two separate songs were fused together for this composition: Stills' 'Know You Got To Run' and Young's 'Everybody I Love You'. What emerged was a fast paced, vibrant finale to this much loved album. In the final 30 seconds or so, Young receives a salutary lesson from CS&N and is buried beneath their vocal power. Stills blues phrasing and Crosby/Nash's skyward harmonies interfuse in what can only be described as an almost too perfect studio creation, culminating in what sounds like a full blown church organ. As a wilful practitioner of the imperfect, Young failed to appreciate the technical and emotional strengths that the superstar trio brought to his songs. Despite all his later genre experimentation, he never returned to the full scale Spectoresque productions that characterised his now severely and unfairly underrated work with CS&N.

Full track listing: Carry On; Teach Your Children; Almost Cut My Hair; Helpless; Woodstock; Déjà Vu; Our House; 4+20; Country Girl; Everybody I Love You.

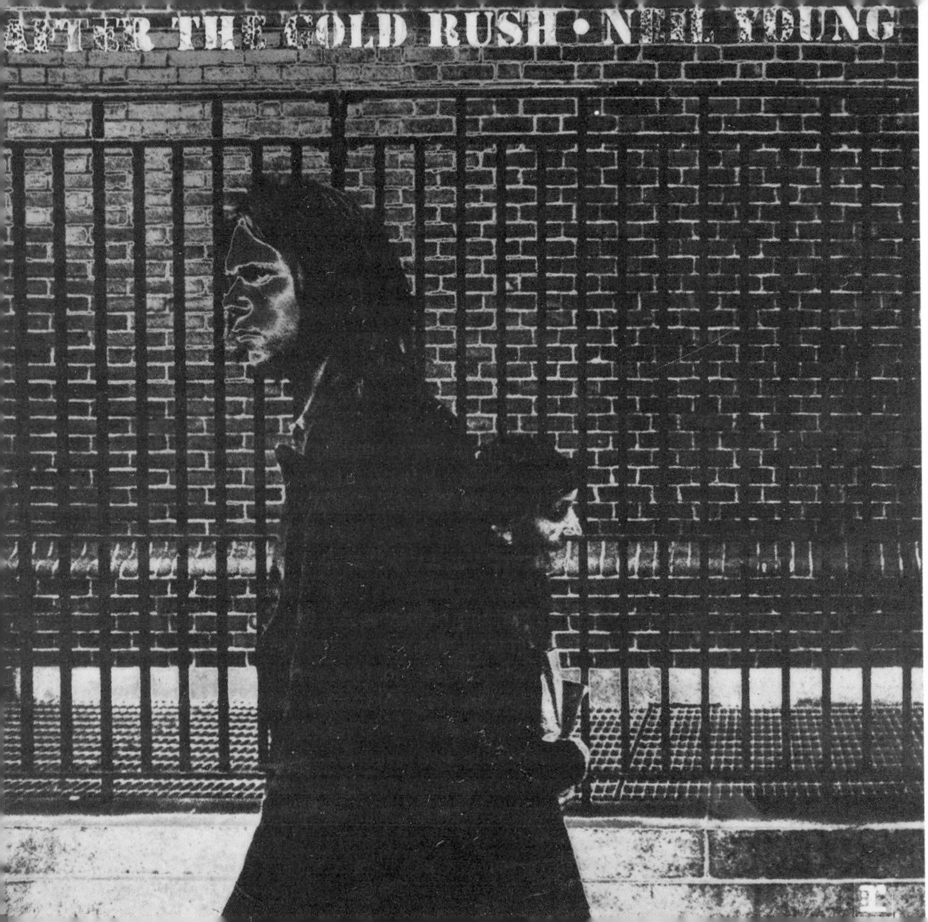
AFTER THE GOLD RUSH • NEIL YOUNG

AFTER THE GOLDRUSH

ORIGINAL RELEASE DATE: AUGUST 1970

Young took another unexpected turn of direction on his third album, jettisoning Crazy Horse due to guitarist Danny Whitten's increasing drug dependency. In the end, the work was pieced together at Young's home studio in Topanga Canyon with new find Nils Lofgren as right hand man on piano/guitar. "I didn't know much about Neil, apart from the fact that he was once in The Buffalo Springfield," Lofgren explained. "I'd never really heard his songs but our writing was similar in many ways." Lofgren added stability and enthusiasm to the sessions and gradually Young invited other old friends to contribute including Ralph Molina, the ostracised Whitten, Stephen Stills and Jack Nitzsche. Although the title of the album was based on a screenplay by Dean Stockwell, the idea of producing a concept work was never realised. Instead Young recorded the album with extraordinary rapidity capturing the spirit of the moment in a series of songs, including ballads, a guitar epic, a country cover and a couple of fragments that serve as tail pieces. It was nevertheless a cohesive work that was generally regarded as the most attractive and influential singer/songwriter album of its time. Even two decades on, it retains much of its original power and charm and many still regard it as one of Young's most notable achievements. Crosby, Stills & Nash had introduced Young to an international audience and now he was taking full advantage of that patronage. During the early CSN&Y concerts he had seemed a mysterious figure, less rounded in press profiles but consistently respected. With this album he demonstrated to an expectant world that he was rock's equivalent to a Romantic poet. His work was commercial but not as sweet or slick as that of emerging rivals like James Taylor. The lyrics were enigmatic and bursting with metaphor and, to top it all, he was clearly a guitar hero, right up there with Stephen Stills. The notion of Neil Young as cult celebrity was born here.

TELL ME WHY

The influence of CS&N continued on this track, with Nils Lofgren providing the harmony and additional guitar work. Sweet melancholy is the dominant theme with a dash of suitably poetic imagery in the description of "heart ships" sailing through "broken harbours". Young's vocal is confident and the diction precise as he finds the perfect persona for the singer-songwriter age. Young claims that he ceased performing the song after a while because the self-questioning lyrics sounded too intense.

AFTER THE GOLDRUSH

Switching to piano, Young sings in his highest register here, valiantly attempting to stay in tune throughout. The lyrics are intriguing, possibly Young's best up until this point. Over three verses he presents a dream sequence, switching from medieval times ("the knights in armour saying something about a queen") to the present day and finally to a futuristic utopian vision of "silver spaceships... flying Mother Nature's new-born seed to a new home..." The apocalyptic theme bore more than a passing resemblance to Crosby's post-nuclear prophecy 'Wooden Ships' which, coincidentally, was also planned as a film. One interesting footnote to 'After The Goldrush' is that it was twice a hit in the UK for vocal group Prelude.

ONLY LOVE CAN BREAK YOUR HEART

This melodic ballad gave Young his first US Top 40 hit, climbing to number 33 in December 1970. Both the phrasing and the diction are impressive and Young cleverly walks a tightrope between composing a commercial song and a convincing singer-songwriter confessional piece. At the time, it was rumoured that the subject of the song was Stephen Stills, but Young later revealed that it was directed at Graham Nash, who was then in the throes of a love affair with Joni Mitchell. Ironically, Stills did later record the song.

SOUTHERN MAN

Returning to the Crazy Horse tradition of guitar epics, Young established himself among the axe-men of his era with this fiercely wrought piece. While damning the institutionalised racialism of the South, Young reaches a froth of indignation, culminating in the harrowing third verse in which he steps directly into the narrative and adopts the persona of the persecutor, screaming, "I've seen your black man coming round/Swear by God I'm gonna cut him down". It was small wonder that this became the highlight of his live set during the early Seventies. The song's popularity was underlined in the most bathetic way imaginable when The Dave Clark Five released a cover version as a single.

TILL THE MORNING COMES

After the intensity of 'Southern Man', Young offers some light relief with this brief refrain which is most memorable for its surprise trumpet solo.

OH LONESOME ME

The first cover version released by Young was this disappointing reading of the Don Gibson classic. During the same period, Young was considering the possibility of recording a country album and this sounds suspiciously like an outtake from that unrealized project. It also revealed the first signs of his artistic perversity, summed up in his comments on the song:

"I like it because everybody else seems to hate it so much."

DON'T LET IT BRING YOU DOWN

A perennial concert favourite, this urban drama was composed during Young's visit to London with CS&N in 1970. It was rightly regarded as one of Young's better songs of the period. Although he attempts to paint a realistic portrait of poverty in the city, the chorus is an uplifting distraction from the gloom. He would return to the same theme in more aggressive mood with 'Crime In The City (Sixty To Zero Part 1)'.

BIRDS

This plaintive ballad uneasily attempted to use bird imagery to describe the natural fragmentation of a relationship. Young regarded the song as too personal to feature regularly in performance, but apparently voiced no reservations about its inclusion on the album. It's been suggested that the closing words of the song ('It's Over') may be a veiled tribute to Roy Orbison but the execution reveals none of the neurotic drama for which the Big O was renowned. An alternate take of the song borrowed from an earlier session can be heard on the B-side of the single 'Only Love Can Break Your Heart'.

WHEN YOU DANCE I CAN REALLY LOVE

The combination of dancing and sexuality reaches an exuberant pitch half-way through this song when Young excitedly exclaims: "I can love; I can really love". The realisation sends him stumbling towards some embarrassingly lazy similes ("Like a mountain that's growing/A river that rolls"), while Jack Nitzsche plays some rollicking piano. It's not Young at his best but effectively breaks up the slower-paced material on the latter half of this album.

I BELIEVE IN YOU

This is the closest Young came to composing an MOR ballad during this relatively early stage of his career. Rita Coolidge gave it the full sultry treatment on her début album, while Young's version is more lugubrious with a relatively sparse arrangement. Reflecting on its lyrics, Young noted: "What am I talking about?... 'Now that you've made yourself love me, do you think I can change it in a day?' That's a heavy one. That song has the most haunting lyrics. 'Am I lying to you when I say I believe in you?'; that's the difference between the song and the poem. The song makes you think of the hook, and the hook is 'I believe in you', but the rest of it is in a whole other place".

CRIPPLE CREEK FERRY

Young closes the album on a playful note in striking contrast to either 'Cowgirl In The Sand' or 'Last Trip To Tulsa'. Here he takes what seems a fragment of a song and uses it as an amusing postscript.

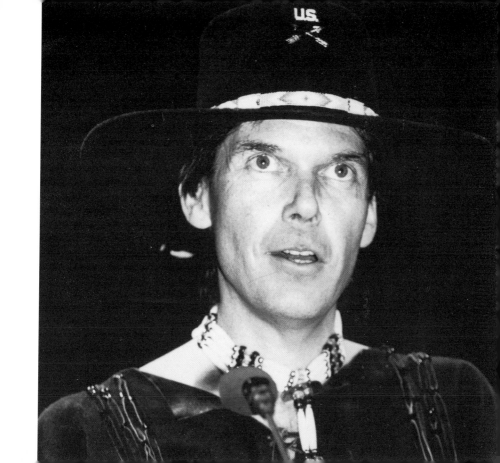

4 WAY STREET

ORIGINAL RELEASE DATE: APRIL 1971

Young had already emerged as the most popular and critically acclaimed member of CSN&Y by the time this live album was issued. Not surprisingly, he gained most of the critical plaudits that were handed out. One review announced categorically: "Young dominates what is more a one-way street." The evident bias was not matched by the material which clearly showed that the other three were far from dormant. Against all odds, it was Crosby & Nash who performed the only previously unissued songs in the set. Young was well represented but there were no new compositions for fans to savour. Instead, we were treated to some intriguing rearrangements of older material as Young adapted to his new role as a purveyor of CS&N-style "wooden music". Buffalo Springfield's now dated pop version of 'On The Way Home' became a favourite opening number, fitting unobtrusively into his acoustic repertoire. Even more surprising was 'Cowgirl In The Sand' now translated from electric epic glory into a compact ballad. By contrast, the recent 'Don't Let It Bring You Down' replicated the mood of the studio version.

On the electric side, Young contributed a far longer version of 'Southern Man' than the one on 'After The Goldrush'. His jams with Stills seemed over indulgent, though it should be remembered that such extended workouts were then all the rage. Completing the Young contributions on the original disc was 'Ohio', already issued as a single and rightly acclaimed as the peak of CSN&Y's achievement. The live version could not hope to match the economy and emotional intensity of the original but nevertheless provided some indication of the power of the composition when played live.

When '4 Way Street' was finally issued on compact disc, several new acoustic tracks were added, including Young's engaging medley of 'The Loner/Cinnamon Girl/Down By The River'. As a memento of the quartet's illustrious indoor concerts of 1970, this package retains an enduring charm.

Full track listing: Suite: Judy Blue Eyes; On The Way Home; Teach Your Children; Triad; The Lee Shore; Chicago; Right Between The Eyes; Cowgirl In The Sand; Don't Let It Bring You Down; 49 Bye Byes/America's Children; Love The One You're With; Pre-Road Downs; Long Time Gone; Southern Man; Ohio; Carry On; Find The Cost Of Freedom.

HARVEST

ORIGINAL RELEASE DATE: FEBRUARY 1972

This was the album that changed Young's standing in the rock world to a degree that seemed unimaginable. It spawned a chart-topping single and reached number 1 in the album charts on both sides of the Atlantic. Suddenly, Young was catapulted to a level of fame that momentarily eclipsed even that of Crosby, Stills & Nash. Mainstream critical reaction was reasonably favourable, but more discriminating commentators were clearly concerned by what seemed a drop in standards. *Rolling Stone* argued: "... it can only be concluded that Neil Young is not one of those folks whom superstardom becomes artistically. 'Harvest', a painfully long year-plus in the making... finds Young invoking most of the LA variety of superstardom's weariest clichés in an attempt to obscure his inability to do a good imitation of his earlier self." The reviewer concluded that Young "still sings awful pretty, and often even touchingly. For the most part, though, he's seemingly lost sight of what once made his music uniquely compelling and evocative and become just another pretty-singing solo superstar."

Such reservations were understandable but told only part of the story. It may be that Young was consciously aiming for a larger audience but, in many respects, his new "laid-back" style was thrust upon him by a back injury which prevented him from playing electric guitar or exerting himself to any great degree. Viewed from a distance *Harvest* can now be seen as simply another facet of Young's musical personality, representing that part of him which is most commercial, sentimental and therefore occasionally cloying. It's a less accomplished work than its three predecessors but its predominant songs of sweet melancholy retain a superficial charm and are very well-crafted and difficult to dislike. Equally importantly, the album enabled Young to put together another group, The Stray Gators, whose membership would be called upon for related projects in the future.

OUT ON THE WEEKEND

Young's mood of laid-back star-weariness has seldom been better expressed than in the opening lines of this composition: "Think I'll pack it in and buy a pick-up". The song, taken at mid-pace, is restlessly ambivalent, with the lyrics optimistically proclaiming the emergence of a "brand new day", while Young adds the qualification, "I'm so down today". Reflecting on the song's theme, he realised that there was a happy ending in there somewhere that he had subconsciously suppressed: "I really say I'm happy in the second part of that verse. I say I'm completely happy by saying 'can't relate to joy... tries to speak and can't begin to say'. That just means that I'm so happy that I can't get it out. But it doesn't sound happy. The way I wrote it sounds sad."

HARVEST

The title track is another light tune in which the pedal steel backing brightens a series of rhetorical questions alluding to a seemingly idealised relationship. The harvest image refers to the narrator's reflections on the amount of love he is likely to receive and whether he can take such beneficence.

A MAN NEEDS A MAID

For most listeners this was the most striking melody on the album. The song was inspired by his relationship with actress Carrie Snodgress, soon to be the mother of his first child. Some commentators were distracted by the apparent chauvinistic connotations of the title although it seems clear from the first verse that the lyrics are more concerned with the narrator's insecurity. Unfortunately, Young did himself no favours by omitting these lines from the lyric sheet. What should have been one of his most haunting songs was fatally compromised by the decision to bury the sentiments beneath an avalanche of orchestration. As Young noted: "Some people thought this arrangement was overdone but Bob Dylan told me it was one of his favourites. I listened closer to Bob".

HEART OF GOLD

Young called this the song that "put me in the middle of the road". Its ascent to number 1 in the US charts confirmed his standing as the most commercial singer songwriter of the year, with all its attendant expectations. When Bob Dylan heard the song on the radio he was mightily miffed at the Canadian's supposed assimilation of his vocal style. Actually, it doesn't sound particularly like Dylan, but is a strong track in its own right with some excellent additional vocals from James Taylor and Linda Ronstadt.

ARE YOU READY FOR THE COUNTRY?

The title was a pertinent question for his audience and the answer was undoubtedly divided. Some assumed that Young was riding the times and taking advantage of the burgeoning country rock boom, but the music was to become a familiar part of his repertoire over the years, through 'American Stars 'n Bars', 'Comes A Time', 'Old Ways' and 'Harvest Moon'.

OLD MAN

Inspired by his ranch-hand Louis Avila, who was then in his late sixties, this song reflected on the common needs of those separated by two generations. When Scott Young, Neil's father, heard the song played live he mistakenly assumed that it had been written about him. The track, one of Young's better tunes of the period, provided his third and last US Top 40 hit single to date.

THERE'S A WORLD

This slight song suffered the full bombastic weight of the London Symphony Orchestra and ended up sounding like a parody of classical rock. It's difficult not to be distracted by the flutes, harps and violins that attempt to make Young sound like a cross between Mozart and Wagner.

ALABAMA

One of the stronger songs on the album, this saw Young returning to the 'Southern Man' theme, albeit in a less angry tone. Crosby & Nash's harmony work adds a new dimension to the track proving that the old partnership still had a lot to offer. The sentiments of the song were not appreciated by everybody and prompted Lynyrd Skynyrd to compose their memorable riposte 'Sweet Home Alabama', which Young generously applauded.

THE NEEDLE AND THE DAMAGE DONE

Danny Whitten's lapse into heroin addiction inspired this bittersweet lament for the Crazy Horse guitarist. Moving but also worryingly sentimental with its inappropriate "setting sun" imagery, it displayed Young's initial sympathetic response to the plight of the junkie. Later compositions in the same vein would show his darker side in all its sordid glory.

The song was a favourite choice as a B-side for Young singles and backed the otherwise unavailable 'War Song', the sole example of a recording credited to Neil Young and Graham Nash.

WORDS

With its pastoral imagery and sardonic reflections on superstar life, this song looked better on paper than it sounded on record. Stills and Nash are on hand to add some harmonic touches but the tune never quite lives up to expectations despite some interesting moments. Who could have guessed that the same song would take up 25 per cent of Young's next album?

JOURNEY THROUGH THE PAST

ORIGINAL RELEASE DATE: NOVEMBER 1972

While at the peak of his fame Young issued this disastrous double album which was universally condemned as the ultimate in artistic indulgence. It might have been better tolerated had it been stressed that it was not a Young release but a film soundtrack. Unfortunately, Warner Brothers promoted the work as though it was the follow-up to 'Harvest'. The movie became one of rock's best kept secrets and was actually banned in the UK as a result of its explicit depiction of a junkie injecting heroin into his arm. Even if everybody had seen the film, the soundtrack would hardly have made sense of it all. As Young correctly observed, "It's got no plot. No point. No stars. They don't want to see that."

The soundtrack began with some snatches of archive material from The Buffalo Springfield, followed by CSN&Y performing 'Find The Cost Of Freedom' and 'Ohio'. The last was a strong version but coming so soon after '4 Way Street' its impact was lessened. The same could be said of the live 'Southern Man'. Some of the rehearsals from 'Harvest' were of passing interest, but 16 minutes of a desultory version of 'Words' strained the listener's patience to breaking point. The final quarter of the album hardly featured Young at all. Instead, we were greeted by the Tony & Susan Alamo Christian Foundation Orchestra & Chorus performing Handel's *Messiah* and *King Of Kings* and The Beach Boys' instrumental 'Let's Go Away For Awhile'. Those in search of new Young material were left with a paltry one song, 'Soldier', which was poorly recorded and unmemorable.

At the time, the soundtrack album seemed a typical example of crass exploitation either aimed at completists who would buy anything or innocents naïvely seeking another 'Harvest'. On another level, the album was a first salvo in Young's demythologising of his stardom. And there would be more shocks to come.

Full track listing: For What It's Worth; Mr Soul; Rock & Roll Woman; Find The Cost Of Freedom; Ohio; Southern Man; Are You Ready For The Country?; Let Me Call You Sweetheart; Alabama; Words; God Bless America; Relativity Invitation; Handel's Messiah; King Of Kings; Soldier; Let's Go Away For Awhile.

TIME FADES AWAY

ORIGINAL RELEASE DATE: SEPTEMBER 1973

The circumstances surrounding the recording of this live album were bizarre, even by Young's standards. At first he put together a variety of musicians, including members of The Stray Gators and Crazy Horse, including Jack Nitzsche and Danny Whitten. During rehearsals, Whitten's drug dependence became painfully apparent and Young was left with no choice but to fire his friend. As a parting gesture he gave Whitten $50 which the guitarist used to score some heroin. Later that same night, Young was told that Whitten was dead from a drugs overdose.

The ill-fated tour went ahead but it seemed cursed by the ghost of Whitten and stumbled from one crisis to the next. There was mutiny among the road crew, who demanded more of the box office money, much to Young's chagrin. On-stage the playing gradually became more ragged and finally Young's voice gave out. By the closing stages of the tour he was reduced to screaming out hoarsely and berating audiences for their complacency. A distress signal was sent to Crosby & Nash who responded by joining the tour and adding some much needed harmonies. Nothing could distract from the shambolic nature of the performances though and many were left wondering about Young's state of mind in the wake of his superstar success.

That he would sanction a live album of the tour indicated either eccentricity or suggested that he lacked the songs to follow up 'Harvest'. In fact, neither was the case. Young deliberately included an album full of previously unreleased songs. His own interpretation of the work was that he simply felt the need to document as nakedly as possible "where I was truly at". Judging from much of the album, that place was in the pits of despair, among the junkies, street people and hangers-on. The mood of the album is aggressive, petulant, self-questioning and sometimes downright belligerent. Musically, the songs and performances are erratic but there is a courageousness there that is impressive. Critical reaction to the album was scathing at the time, with one headline proclaiming "Neil Young Fades Away". For long-term fans, though, it was a benchmark release. If you got through this one and appreciated the undoubted jewels in the rough, then you were more than ready to follow Young through one of the most fascinating and rewarding periods of his career.

TIME FADES AWAY

Bar-room piano and a queasy harmonica style are the appropriate musical accompaniment to Young's tale of junkies and politicians, set incongruously against a repetitive plea to "be home by eight". By the final verse, there is a temporal shift as the action reverts to the Canada of Young's youth and its effects upon his outlook. Overall, it's a fascinating insight to a previously unknown side of Young that is now all too familiar.

JOURNEY THROUGH THE PAST

Young continues his speculation on days past with this already familiar song. Alas, this rough version pales alongside the more restrained

reading that he gave the song in concert during 1971. On reading the song's title many listeners must have wondered why it wasn't included on the flimsy film soundtrack of the same name.

YONDER STANDS THE SINNER

This was another of Young's sardonic attacks on institutionalised religion, sung in his most off-key voice to date. It sounds like little more than an improvised blues, but neatly captures the shambolic nature of the show. In the song Young lampoons the coercive paternalistic morality of the Church by portraying himself as a naughty child: "Well I was about as scared as I could be/I went and hid behind the nearest tree/Peaked out from behind the branches/Sinner!" Given the context, one might expect the chorus to read: " 'Yonder stands the sinner'/He calls my name without a sound". But Young drops the single inverted commas thereby altering the meaning. With the speech marks included, Young would be under verbal attack as the sinner, but by removing them the meaning is reversed so that it is the moraliser who is cast in the role as sinner: "Yonder

stands the sinner/He [the sinner] calls my name without a sound". The entire song is engagingly ironic.

LA

Written as early as 1968, this was Young's fantasy vision of the destruction of Los Angeles. There is an underlying glee in his apocalyptic vision that is both intriguing and disconcerting.

LOVE IN MIND

Here is a melody that would not have been out of place on either of Young's two previous studio albums. It's written in the old confessional singer-songwriter style, complete with a romantic subplot and yet another stab at religious values ("Churches long preach sex is wrong/Jesus where is nature going"). Among the other more raucous tracks it sounds strangely out of place, recalling a persona that already seems past.

DON'T BE DENIED

Even those who conservatively decried the coarseness of this record had to admit that this was a major achievement. It's Young's

autobiography spread over four verses in which he details his parents' marital break-up, the formation of The Squires, the sudden success of The Buffalo Springfield in Hollywood and, finally, the spiritual emptiness of fame. The chorus reiterates the need to grasp the moment, as Young has so often done. It's worth noting that there are other versions of this song on the tour that feature an extra verse, regrettably absent from this nevertheless inspired recording.

THE BRIDGE

Inspired by the Hart Crane poem of the same name, this short song, with minimal piano and harmonica accompaniment, served as a reflective and highly erotic interlude between the two epics that closed the album.

LAST DANCE

A burst of feedback opens this momentous and contentious composition, while Young's off-key vocals bounce off against an uncertain accompaniment. At times it almost seems as though the recording is running too slowly, until Young takes matters into his own hands with a guitar solo that stretches across the song and brings the other instruments together in a solid groove. Lyrically, it harks back to the *carpe diem* philosophy of 'Don't Be Denied' as Young urges the audience to "live your own life/laid back and laughing". The sentiments are condescending and by the time he visualises the grind and pointlessness of Monday morning, his voice takes on a discernibly mocking tone. It's a slap in the face to the same people whom he irreverently admonished to "wake up" at other shows.

Lest we condemn him for his patronising arrogance there is a get-out clause in the coda in which he questions all his self-righteous advice with the desperate refrain, "No! No! No!" Guest vocalist Crosby implores the audience to chant along before the song collapses in on itself. It remains one of those unquestionably great moments in the Young canon, all the more so because it's not from an album that instantly jumps on to your playlist.

ON THE BEACH

ORIGINAL RELEASE DATE: JULY 1974

Following 'Time Fades Away', Young undertook another controversial tour but the attendant album, 'Tonight's The Night', was put on hold. Instead, Young issued this remarkable record which remains, in many respects, the pinnacle of his achievement as a singer-songwriter. At the time, it received a cautiously favourable review in *Rolling Stone* which concluded: "'On The Beach' is one of the most despairing albums of the decade, a bitter testament from one who has come through the fire and gone back into it." Others critics were less sympathetic and saw the album simply as another downer from a writer who had lost his melodic edge. For those who had seen merit in Young's 'Time Fades Away' however, the album clearly represented something far more substantial. Critic Ian MacDonald was among this small group and took the unusual step of penning a lengthy reappraisal of the album not long after one of his colleagues at the *NME* had panned the work in an aggressive review. MacDonald's contention was that 'On The Beach' was a watershed in Young's career and a timely rejection of the prevailing values of LA superstar life. As MacDonald argued: "Young has earned a reasonable living out of making some successful artistic statements (for money) about sensations we all feel at one time or other. 'I'm miserable but I can make it sound pretty with my songs' pays 'I like to hum along to your songs about misery 'cos I probably quite fancy it myself'. Like Leonard Cohen. A sugared pill just the correct distance into commerciality to still be believable... And that could be the main reason why the majority of Neil Young fans won't get into 'On The Beach'. The pill is no longer sugared – either by Sweet Melody or by garlands of posies. Instead, three varieties of twelve-bar, one real primitive back country number and lines like 'You're all just pissing in the wind'... Young has quite simply welshed on the deal. Which, in turn, suggests he's Woken Up... 'On The Beach' isn't, as previously interpreted, the fag-end of

Neil Young's romance with rejection, but actually a quite positive piece of work in the Merciless Realism bracket of Lennon's primal period".

Such a review was tantamount to a call to arms for those caught up in this uncertain but fascinating phase of Young's career. The album took the pain and uncertainty witnessed on Young's last two tours and distilled from it a work of astonishing vision. Here was Young both analysing his past like a man three times his age and offering a fresh perspective on his future. The work reached a memorable climax in its final three songs which took up an entire side of the vinyl album. As a mood piece this segment is arguably unsurpassed in the Young canon and, like the album as a whole, stands valiantly apart from the main body of the songwriter's work.

WALK ON

After the intensity of the past year-and-a-half, Young opens the album on a stoical, upbeat note, proclaiming: "sooner or later it all gets real". The song analyses his relationship with the world and focuses on his public persona as the introspective singer-songwriter. "Oo,

baby, that's so hard to change", he says of his familiar role in the rock world, while the refrain 'Walk On' indicates the continued process of change. As Young said of the song: "My own defensive reactions to criticisms of 'Tonight's The Night' and the seemingly endless flow of money coming from you people out there."

SEE THE SKY ABOUT TO RAIN

This song was already familiar to audiences who had witnessed his acoustic shows in 1971. More recently, The Byrds had included the song on their reunion album. Young's new version is a subdued affair and seemingly out of place with the remainder of the work, which features entirely new songs. Nevertheless, its fatalistic point of view echoes the sentiments of 'Walk On'.

REVOLUTION BLUES

Writing a satire based on Charles Manson might not be the most tasteful of ideas, but Young invests the song with a scathing humour, portraying the protagonists as crazed outlaws who ironically employ the symbols of the peace and love movement ("Yes, that was me with the doves/Setting them free near the factory"). The Manson allusions become explicit towards the end of the song with the horrific image of the "bloody fountains", but there is a subtle shift as Young implicitly places himself among the targets. Although this song might seem an unlikely stage number for CSN&Y, it featured frequently in their stadium concerts while Crosby contributed rhythm guitar to the studio recording. Given the criticisms levelled at Young for his supposedly "depressing" material, it is worth remembering violinist/guitarist Rusty Kershaw's happy, semi-literate, footnotes on the song. Although uncredited as a musician on the track, he obviously played his part: "On 'Revolution Blues' I turned into a python than (sic) an aligator (sic), I was crawling like one makeing (sic) noises like one. Plus I was eating up the carpit (sic) and mike stands and such and in the meanwhile I started to crawl up towards Neil; which is pretty spookky (sic) when your (sic) trying to sing. But anyways by that time the neck tie people ask my friend Joe, "what are you gonna do about Rusty", and my friends answere (sic) was Hell I don't know I'm just hanging around to see if he'll swallow him or not."

FOR THE TURNSTILES

Here, Young presents an analogy between the fates of baseball players and rock stars as a comment on his own career. The song gets to the heart of the artist's neurosis – how to effect change in the mummifying arena of rock stardom. This was one of two songs on the album co-produced by David Briggs. Young's vocal sounds more polished here, while the banjo accompaniment complements the reflective mood.

VAMPIRE BLUES

This plodding blues is rescued by a throbbing, if tentative, lead guitar break. Once again, Young's satirical intent is present, this time in his adoption of the persona of a blood-sucking oil magnate. The connection between oil barons and the record industry gives the song a sharper edge.

Note also the surprise appearance of guitarist George Whitsell, a former member of Crazy Horse predecessors, The Rockets.

ON THE BEACH

The second half of the album features some of the best material Young ever wrote. In this song, he questions the nature of fame and its impact upon his mental state. A slow, precise guitar solo cuts through the prevarication as Young attempts to resolve his sense of inertia. Intense images of isolation are ever present but the meditation ends with decisive action, even if it is a trip into the unknown ("I head for the sticks with my bus and friends/I travel a road though I don't know where it ends"). One of the surprising features of this track is the unique presence of a veritable gallery of musicians from Young's past, including Stray Gator Ben Keith, Crazy Horse's Ralph Molina and, representing the CS&N camp, Graham Nash.

MOTION PICTURES

This stoned reverie, written after ingesting copious amounts of marijuana, was ostensibly a tribute to Young's actress wife, Carrie Snodgress. On closer inspection though, it's another contemplation on the state of his career, closing with the defiant riposte: 'I'd rather start all over again". Although the sentiments are ultimately celebratory, the self-analytical questioning and drug-induced lethargy give the composition a melancholic air. As

Young reminded us, he often sounds at his saddest when singing his happiest songs.

AMBULANCE BLUES

The album closes with this extraordinary examination of Young's career. Unlike 'Don't Be Denied', this is not straight autobiography but an oblique, sometimes labyrinthine journey into the songwriter's history and psyche. He sets the scene "back in the old folky days", long before his arrival in the USA. At first, this seems straightforward nostalgia ("The air was magic when we played") but the narrative rapidly takes on an elegiacal edge as Young relates the demolition of the street where he lived ("Isabella"), confronts us with wailing waitresses, burn-outs and even a black fairy tale ("Old Mother Goose, she's on the skids"). The ambulance motif is employed as a means to overcome the career crises that grip the artiste who is too tied to a familiar pattern. At times Young himself appears to get lost in the complex lyrical spider's web ("It's hard to tell the meaning of this song") but midway through he is confident enough to proclaim: "I guess I'll call it sickness gone". In one wonderfully defiant moment, he attempts to turn the tables on his critics by comparing their achievements with his own. The tone is not petulant, but playful to the point of camaraderie ("We could get together for some scenes"). By the end of the song, the allusions become more topical. There's a passing reference to Elliot Roberts' dictum, "You're just pissing in the wind" and what is generally accepted as a sly dig at Richard Nixon in the closing lines

("I never knew a man could tell so many lies"). Throughout, the acoustic instrumentation focuses attention on the lyrics, while Kershaw's fiddle enhances the dramatic breaks between verses. This was the summit of Young's achievement as a singer songwriter and remains the most likely candidate as his greatest and most memorable composition.

SO FAR

ORIGINAL RELEASE DATE: JULY 1974

When CSN&Y reconvened in 1974 for their celebrated stadium tour, their record company and fans were crying out for new product. The foursome declined the opportunity to record a new album, much to everyone's frustration, and so this compilation was hastily issued. It warrants a mention here for two reasons: first, it was a number 1 album and is available on CD; second, it featured the single version of Young' s 'Ohio', a composition that is crucially important in any discussion of CSN&Y.

Those two features notwithstanding, there is little else to recommend the collection. The idea of releasing a compilation album from an act that had only recorded a single studio album as a foursome and another as a trio (minus Young) was stretching the meaning of the album title to absurd lengths. None of the four took the project seriously and were clearly embarrassed by its existence, although its chart performance must have been gratifying for all. At least Joni Mitchell provided some originality by providing the artwork.

OHIO

CSN&Y'S greatest moment on record was this moving anthem dedicated to the four students killed by the National Guard at Kent State University on 4 May 1970. At the time Young seemed an apolitical creature but it was difficult to sit on the fence amid the ever present liberal radicalism of CS&N. Crosby, one of the great proselytizers in rock, was the catalyst in encouraging Young to react to the Kent State killings. He even gave him *Time* magazine's report of the event and watched solicitously as Young rapidly wrote the composition. Its sentiments were uncompromising and finger-pointing ("Tin soldiers and Nixon's coming/We're finally on our own/This summer I hear the drumming/Four dead in Ohio"). CSN&Y, at that point scattered, immediately reconvened in LA and recorded the song, which was backed by Stills' 'Find The Cost Of Freedom'. Using their power and influence at Atlantic, CSN&Y ensured that the record was in the shops by the following week. The single still sounds staggering with Young's searing guitar work illuminating a brilliant live performance which concludes with Crosby screaming "How many more? Why?" with such passion that he can barely hold back the tears. This unforgettable moment underlined everything that CSN&Y meant at their peak.

Full track listing: Déjà Vu; Helplessly Hoping; Wooden Ships; Teach Your Children; Ohio; Find The Cost Of Freedom; Woodstock; Our House; Helpless; Guinnevere; Suite: Judy Blue Eyes.

NEIL YOUNG
TONIGHT'S THE NIGHT

TONIGHT'S THE NIGHT

ORIGINAL RELEASE DATE: JUNE 1975

The contents of this album came as no surprise to those who had witnessed Young's unforgettable and controversial shows in the winter of 1973. Most spectators turned up expecting highlights from *Harvest* but instead they were greeted by the sight of a shambling, tequila-drinking shaman, mumbling about being on Miami Beach and singing barely formed songs in an off-key voice. In London, he played no less than three versions of 'Tonight's The Night' without a word of explanation. At the end of this segment he would urge the audience to "keep on singing", although most of them were already reduced to stony silence. The reviews were unforgiving, heaping praise upon support group The Eagles and more or less dismissing Young as a spent force. At best, he resembled a leading candidate for rock's next major casualty.

The shows might have made a lot more sense at the time if Young had conducted some interviews explaining the circumstances leading up to the creation of these alcohol-fuelled lamentations. Unfortunately, few people were aware of the deaths of Young's associates Danny Whitten and Bruce Berry nor the effects that their drug abuse had on Young. He was shocked into writing a series of songs which took form during late night sessions with Crazy Horse (aka the Santa Monica Flyers) at Studio Instrument Rentals in LA. As bassist Billy Talbot explained: "He wrote it in the studio at SIR – the rehearsal place where we recorded the album. He wrote it just sitting at home that night and the next day we started playing it and it took us about a week to get the first side. We would just get drunk and smoke and so on and then we'd play some more and then we'd go home. We kept doing that all week until one night we just caught about four or five tunes out of one set and then we started realising what the album was really all about. That feeling that we had was so different, it was like a wake... an Irish wake."

The resulting album was so scabrous and bleak that neither Young nor his record company felt ready to place it before the public, especially after the similarly intense 'Time Fades Away'. Instead, it lay buried for two years while Young's career took an upturn with the wildly acclaimed CSN&Y stadium tour. As a follow-up to 'On The Beach', Young had produced a more melodic work titled 'Homegrown' which was set for release then cancelled at the eleventh hour. During a playback party at Rick Danko's house, a tape of 'Tonight's The Night' was played and, with the drink flowing, those in attendance suggested that Young should release this crazed wake instead. Characteristically, he took their advice and almost two years after those strange shows the world heard this remarkable album. Young undertook some keen promotion for the record, perhaps as a damage limitation exercise, for he must have realised that it wouldn't sell in vast quantities. What it achieved was worth far more than record sales for it confirmed Young's reputation as the most uncompromising songwriter/performer of his generation. The album was probably the most moving and harrowing work of his career and a record that sounded both chilling and intriguing when played in the still of night. It added a completely new and rewarding dimension to Young's music. Along with 'On The Beach', this album represented a key moment in Seventies rock, perfectly bridging the gap between singer-songwriter angst and the dawn of punk.

TONIGHT'S THE NIGHT

The album begins with a chant that soon develops into an elegy for CSN&Y guitar roadie Bruce Berry. This song was actually written while Young was in the studio and you can sense the drama as he builds up to the close of the first verse when he remembers picking up the phone to learn of his friend's drug-related death. The story in song is given even greater power by the decision to encourage Nils Lofgren to play in the ragged style of the doomed Berry.

SPEAKIN' OUT

Lofgren's guitar work is again in strong evidence here, alongside Ben Keith's strikingly effectively pedal steel. The rough vocal and bleak tone are slightly deceptive here as Young quickly takes solace in parenthood ("You're holding my baby and I'm holding you").

WORLD ON A STRING

A shift of tempo sees Young return to one of his favourite themes: the emptiness of fame and the need for self-realisation. Note how the careful sequencing of the album is designed to lift the listener when the mood appears to be getting too sombre.

BORROWED TUNE

Young sounds at his most wasted here as he sings alone, backed by piano and harmonica. Self doubt is again uppermost in his mind ("I hope that it matters, I'm having my doubts"). As if demonstrating the debilitating effects of the drug culture, Young lapses into self-admitted plagiarism, audaciously pointing out to the listener that the melody is borrowed from The Rolling Stones, although he doesn't actually name 'Lady Jane' in the song.

COME ON BABY
LET'S GO DOWNTOWN

This was a tribute to another heroin casualty, Danny Whitten. Here, Young intensifies the mood by featuring a vintage performance from the Fillmore East in 1970. Hearing Whitten on lead vocal is a poignant reminder of all that was lost to the needle and works even more effectively than would another Young song on the same theme.

MELLOW MY MIND

"Play it loud, but stay in the other room," was Young's advice about listening to this song. It's Young at his most strained and slurred, complete with bum notes and an agonisingly cracked vocal as he attempts to sing the words "railway track". For all that, indeed because of all that, it is one of the most powerful moments on the record. One can only imagine the reactions of Young's record company upon learning that he intended to feature the song in its raw state.

ROLL ANOTHER NUMBER
(FOR THE ROAD)

In a different context, this could have been a contender for *Harvest*, with its jaunty, country air and dominant steel guitar. Instead it becomes a clever pastiche of a former style which Young employs to have a belated dig at Woodstock ("I'm not going back to Woodstock for awhile.../Oh I don't believe I'll be going back that way"). It's interesting to note that the title celebrates drug taking, albeit of the milder kind.

ALBUQUERQUE

The most noticeable feature of this track is how disciplined Young's vocal sounds. It's as if he's sobered up completely, even though the lyrics would have sounded equally appropriate if he had sung them completely out of tune.

NEW MAMA

In common with 'Speakin' Out', this deals with the joys of birth. On this occasion though, the tone is unambiguously celebratory. Crazy Horse provide the close harmonies that we more usually associate with CSN&Y. Indeed, it's easy to imagine the latter featuring this song on an album. In fact, Stephen Stills did record a cover version for his album 'Stills', which was issued during the same period as 'Tonight's The Night'.

LOOKOUT JOE

This salutary warning to GIs returning from the Vietnam War was one of the songs belatedly added to the album long after it was first recorded. Interestingly, the song was actually written during rehearsals for the 'Time Fades Away' tour just before the death of Danny Whitten. Its imagery is harsher and more vio-lent than most of the songs on the album, but the passion evident in performance makes it a suitable choice, with Whitten firmly in mind.

TIRED EYES

As the album nears its close, Young extends the narrative beyond the deaths of Whitten and Berry to take in the tale of another doper friend who was involved in a fatal shooting following a troubled cocaine deal. During the song, Young adopts several different roles and at one point conducts a dialogue with himself ("Well tell me more/I mean was he a heavy doper or was he just a loser?... He tried to do his best...") As Young noted: "All these people they're all in there. That's why there's so much talking on the record!"

TONIGHT'S THE NIGHT – PART II

Young bookends the album with a chunkier refrain of the title track. It brings back memo-ries of those remarkable shows from 1973 when he astonished audiences by singing three full versions of this song at a time when nobody had heard it before.

ZUMA

ORIGINAL RELEASE DATE: NOVEMBER 1975

Within four months of the release of 'Tonight's The Night' another Young album appeared. The critical reception was close to ecstasy for Young was again back with Crazy Horse but this time producing material which was commercial and blessed with hard edges. As Young attested: "My best albums are the ones with Crazy Horse. They're the most fluid. 'Zuma' was a great electric album coming from a place where pop leaves rock'n'roll".

Critics predicted that *Zuma* would be a massive hit but strangely enough chart statistics confirm that the album only reached the same position as 'Tonight's The Night' in the US (number 25) and failed to dent the Top 30 in the UK. Clearly, Young was still far away from the mass acceptance of the 'Harvest' days but 'Zuma' sold well to students and music press readers. It was a strong album but not quite the all-time classic that some maintained at the time. Several ephemerally pretty and exuberant melodies were featured along with some harder-edged songs reinforced by generally impressive guitar work. The presence of 'Cortez The Killer', one of Young's best songs of the decade, distracted attention from some of the weaker moments on the album and garnered universal praise. More importantly, the album confirmed that Young and Crazy Horse were an ongoing, creative collaboration. After Whitten's death and Nils Lofgren's departure for a solo career, it seemed uncertain whether Crazy Horse would tour with Young again but the arrival of guitarist Frank Sampedro confirmed that the chemistry still worked.

DON'T CRY NO TEARS

This simple but irresistible melody was composed way back in Young's adolescence. His first group, The Squires, privately recorded a prototype of the song, at that time titled 'I Wonder'. Later, during Young's attempt to secure a deal with Elektra as a protest folksinger, the tune was resurrected as 'Don't Pity Me Babe' and captured on demo. Here, it retains its old charm but sounds far more commercial and surprisingly contemporary.

DANGER BIRD

The guitar work on this track so impressed Lou Reed that he claimed it was the best he had ever heard. It's certainly Young at his most intense and brooding with Crazy Horse providing strong instrumental accompaniment and singing counter verses to the central narrative. Young uses the fossilised bird as a metaphor for a doomed relationship, offering the forlorn hope in the final verse: "And though these wings have turned to stone/I can fly, fly, fly away".

PARDON MY HEART

With Tim Drummond on bass and Young playing all the other instruments on the track, Crazy Horse's Ralph Molina and Billy Talbot turn their attention to backing vocals. Here is positive proof that the duo are not merely accompanying players but lovers of layered harmonies, recalling their early grounding in doo-wop. The song itself is a strong acoustic ballad and one of the better compositions on the album.

LOOKIN' FOR A LOVE

Produced by Young and Tim Mulligan, this was the obvious single from the album, although it failed to reach the charts. The song's upbeat optimism bears just a tinge of melancholy, recalling Young's easily accessible work on *Harvest*.

BARSTOOL BLUES

This song pre-empted Young's next project – a drunken excursion through American bars. Guitarist Frank Sampedro recalls asking Young to come out for the evening during which they "must have hit every bar in Malibu". The following morning Young called up to say that, "I don't know when I did it but I wrote three songs last night and I woke up sleeping on them". This was one of the results.

STUPID GIRL

Despite the acerbic title and insulting refrain, this was mainly a forthright comment on a girl's inability to forget the past and start anew. The subject was widely assumed to be Joni Mitchell, although this was most likely wishful thinking on the part of an over-imaginative critic. Nobody ever bothered to ask Young why he should feel so aggrieved about his talented contemporary at this point.

DRIVE BACK

The sole occasion on which Young and John Lennon open a song with the same line: "Whatever gets you through the night". The familiar theme of a broken relationship is given added tension by the narrator's sense of triumph and pleasure at his beloved's departure. Musically, the song is striking, with some notable guitar breaks interplaying with a barely audible piano.

CORTEZ THE KILLER

This was the centrepiece of the album and one of Young's most memorable moments with Crazy Horse. The song builds slowly layer upon layer with the guitar work creating a mesmeric effect. During the recording at producer David Briggs' home on Zuma Beach, there was a circuit blow-out resulting in an entire verse of the song being lost on the final tape. Ignoring this technical hitch, the group had played on and at the end of the session, when he was informed of the missing material, Young shrugged: "I never liked that verse anyway!" Lyrically the song is a fascinating example of Young's use of popular mythology and betrays his casual approach to history. Characters remain undeveloped as Young is driven to make the single point about the genocide of the Aztecs. In an extraordinary final verse, he introduces himself and his loved one into the narrative, as if equating his own romantic problems with a nation's loss of innocence.

THROUGH MY SAILS

Originally titled simply 'Sailboat Song', this was a leftover from the aborted CSN&Y sessions in Maui. Indeed, there is some doubt as to whether Young had any right to release this track in the first place. CS&N provide the key-perfect harmonies, while the musical backing features Stills on bass, Young on guitar and Russ Kunkel on drums. It's intriguing to see CSN&Y placed alongside Crazy Horse on successive tracks, especially as the bright mood of this is in such striking contrast to the theme of 'Cortez The Killer'. It's as though Young was spelling out that he could function effectively in both camps if he chose.

LONG MAY YOU RUN

ORIGINAL RELEASE DATE: SEPTEMBER 1976

The idea of Stills & Young combining forces as a duo was initially an attempt to revive the spirit of Buffalo Springfield. Mid-way through the sessions for this album, however, Crosby & Nash were invited to participate and the first CSN&Y studio album since 'Déjà Vu' seemed only months away. Instead, the sessions ended in bitterness and acrimony when Stills & Young abruptly decided to revert to the original concept and erased Crosby & Nash's contributions from the final recording. Public expectations were still high for a Stills/Young teaming, but the results proved terribly anti-climactic. Rather than the expected intense guitar interplay, Stills & Young offered a strangely subdued album of lacklustre songs, mostly inspired by their time in Hawaii. By the time the album was released the collaboration was long dead. A summer tour brought mixed reviews, then ended in farcical fashion when Young drove away after a gig leaving his partner a sarcastic note which read: "Dear Stephen, Funny how some things that start spontaneously end that way. Eat a peach, Neil".

The following tracks are the five that Young composed for the album:

LONG MAY YOU RUN

Young's famous tribute to his hearse opens the album on a buoyant note. The reference to Blind River conjures up memories of Young's period in The Squires while the topical reference to The Beach Boys frequently drew a burst of applause from audiences at his acoustic shows. Like many of the songs on this album, it's lightweight but charming.

MIDNIGHT ON THE BAY

With its sparse backing and reflective but unarresting lyrics, this was obviously an exercise in understatement. Its appeal lies in an attractive melody but it's difficult to believe that Young spent much time on the composition.

OCEAN GIRL

Stills makes his presence felt here with some wah-wah guitar but it's not enough to rescue a fairly inconsequential composition of two short verses. The song sounds undeveloped, as though Young was content to take some fragmentary allusions about drinking cocktails in the sun and attempt to conjure a suitably romantic setting.

LET IT SHINE

Young turns to gospel for a country song that sounds close to a parody. Not for the first time, he passes comment on contemporary religion, but here he can barely muster the usual indignation beyond a sarcastic, "Let them chant, let them chant".

FONTAINEBLEAU

Strangely enough, the most urgent song on the album emerges from Young's almost paranoid loathing of a Miami holiday resort. A reviewer once pondered with some justification why Young should get so upset about a hotel. Perhaps the answer lies in the second verse in which Young explains: "I guess the reason I'm so scared of it is/I stayed there once and I almost fit/I left before I got out of it/People were drowning in their own Fontainebleau". Young's scathing observations inspire some of his familiarly anguished guitar playing, which is certainly rare on this album.

Full track listing: Long May You Run; Midnight On The Bay; Make Love To You; Black Coral; Ocean Girl; Let It Shine; 12/8 Blues (All The Same); Fontainebleau; Guardian Angel.

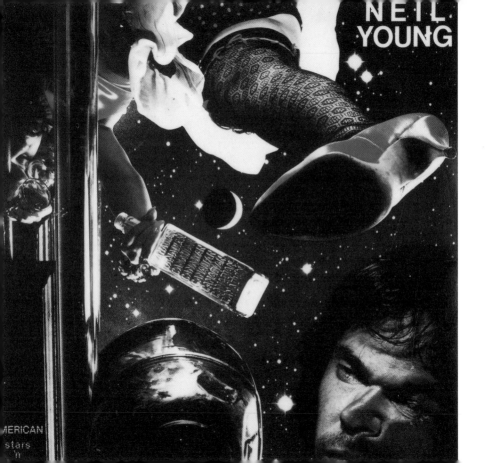

NEIL
YOUNG

AMERICAN
stars
'n

AMERICAN STARS 'N BARS

ORIGINAL RELEASE DATE: JUNE 1977

Thanks to his 1976 world tour with Crazy Horse and highly publicised collaboration with Stills, Young's profile was at its highest since 'Harvest'. This album fared modestly in the US charts but climbed to number 12 in the UK, his highest position as a soloist since 1972. Unfortunately, the contents were not as impressive as the chart figures. Having planned an album under the working title 'Chrome Dreams', Young abruptly decided to produce a more spontaneous work. After recruiting Nicolette Larson and Linda Ronstadt he quickly recorded some rough country songs in April, a mere two months before the album's release. These took up an entire side of the album with the remainder pooled from various older sessions. The result was a terribly uneven work with material so ill-matched that the album lacked any identity at all. Even the long-awaited 'Like A Hurricane' seemed out of place, although its presence alone no doubt prompted heavy sales.

THE OLD COUNTRY WALTZ

Ben Keith's steel guitar and the fiddle of Carole Mayedo are the highlights of this opening foray into country 'n' western. The lyrics are a microcosm of familiar Nashville scenarios: a relationship breaks up while the band are playing an old country waltz and by the last verse the narrator is heading for the Tequila bottle.

SADDLE UP THE PALOMINO

Here, Young introduces us to his horse, Melody. The raucous lyrics include some humorous lines in which he compares the trials of love to a cold bowl of chilli, before adopting the role of a devious adulterer ("It's the neighbour's wife I'm after").

HEY BABE

This song featured the most banal lyrics on the album, but at least there was a good pedal steel backing. It's easy to imagine this being performed as a straight, plaintive love song, but here the arrangement is almost jaunty.

HOLD BACK THE TEARS

Singing in a painfully high register, Young desperately attempts to compete with Linda Ronstadt and Nicolette Larson, whose vocals dominate. The tune has a strong Mexican flavour, with Young dishing out instant aphorisms of encouragement. It's worth noting that a starker version of the song, minus the country embellishments, can be found on an acetate of 'Chrome Dreams', the album that was rumoured for release prior to 'American Stars 'n Bars'. The version featured there is also notable for the inclusion of an additional verse.

BITE THE BULLET

The first half of the album ends on a raucous note with the wailing chorus of Ronstadt and Larson (aka The Bullets). Young even teases his liberal listeners with some amusing macho posturing ("She's a walking love machine/I like to hear her scream") typical of his wry humour.

STAR OF BETHLEHEM

Young reaches back to 1974 for the oldest song on the album. He uses yet another female singer to enrich the harmonies, this time Emmylou Harris. The song details the sense of

loss produced by passing time, while the title uses an agnostic viewpoint to express his own misgivings about love: "Maybe the Star of Bethlehem wasn't a star at all".

WILL TO LOVE

Recorded in 1976 on a two-track Sony cassette recorder, this was the strangest song on the album and one of the oddest in the Young canon. It was conspicuously absent from Young's live shows, a point he stressed to journalist Bill Flanagan: "I never have sung it except for that one time... for the record... I brought two tracks of the cassette up on a couple of faders with the stereo vibrato... then I mixed them in with the original cassette for that sound of fish. I overdubbed all the instruments on it and mixed it in the same night... What a night that was, man, unbelievable. I ordered all the instruments from Studio Instrument Rentals – the drums, the bass, the amps, the vibes, all the percussion stuff. We had them set it up live... I made the transfer of the cassette on to the 16-track and then I started overdubbing all the parts. They thought it was going to be a live session! They were all set up and ready to go. I just walked from one to another and did them all, mostly all on the first take. And then I mixed it at the end of the night. It took us about eight hours to finish the whole thing and make it sound like it does. I think it might be one of the best records I've ever made. I think as a piece of music and sound and lyric and spirit, it's one of the best. And that's why it's important to me as an artist to be able to record a song when I want to."

Lyrically, the song stretched Young's writing powers. Using the painfully extended metaphor of a fish's fight for survival, he documents his own romantic struggles and dreams over seven verses. The convoluted imagery is both frustrating and fascinating as he seriously overreaches himself.

LIKE A HURRICANE

For many this is the apotheosis of the Neil Young/Crazy Horse partnership. Of all the songs he has recorded this was probably the most eagerly anticipated, having been played around the world during his memorable tour of 1976. The sight of Young playing his heart out while a giant electric fan almost blew him into the air is a striking theatrical reminder from those concerts. This studio version lacks the spontaneous power of many of the bootlegged live workouts, but it became a classic FM track and elevated Young to guitar hero status. As he pointed out, though, the playing wasn't flash or pyrotechnic, but hypnotic in the familiar Crazy Horse style: "All it is is four notes on the bass, just keeps going down. Billy plays a few extra notes now and then and the drum beat's the same all the way through. It's like a trance we get into. Sometimes it does sound as if we're playing fast, but we're not. Everything starts swimming around in circles, and everything starts elevating and it transcends the point of playing fast or slow." Indeed the epic quality of the track results from Young's intuitive ability to take each solo into another area rather than repeating a chorus *ad infinitum*.

HOMEGROWN

Not for the first time, Young closes the album on a humorous, anti-climactic note as though he is returning for a quick encore. This was the title track to another album that failed to appear and serves as a double tribute to would-be farmers and marijuana growers of distinction.

DECADE

ORIGINAL RELEASE DATE: NOVEMBER 1977

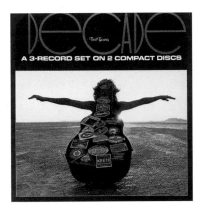

News that Young was compiling a triple album documenting his career seemed a mixed blessing given his wayward tastes. Fortunately, the set proved an impressive sampler of his career (six Springfield cuts; two tracks from 'Neil Young'; three from 'Everybody Knows This Is Nowhere', including the two longest tracks; three from 'After The Goldrush'; two CSN&Y contributions and five from 'Harvest'). Interestingly, he chose only two tracks each from 'Tonight's The Night' and 'On The Beach', plus one from 'Zuma', perhaps preferring to leave those relatively recent albums intact. Reviews of 'Decade' were extremely favourable and for the hard-core fans there were the following half-a-dozen songs previously unavailable on album.

DOWN TO THE WIRE

One of the strongest unreleased Buffalo Springfield cuts, this track was criminally left off 'Last Time Around' where it would have perfectly represented Young *in absentia*. Collectors of unreleased material were already familiar with the song from the bootleg 'Stampede', which also featured a second version sung by Stills.

SUGAR MOUNTAIN

Young's most famous B-side finally finds its way on to an album. The song was written in a hotel in Fort William on the occasion of his nineteenth birthday. The composition is surprisingly child-like for a seemingly mature teenager and contains some of the most trite verses he has ever written. Young himself acknowledged this fact when he played the song in concert at the LA Forum. Despite his previous reluctance to place the track on album it remained a live favourite throughout his career.

WINTERLONG

Originally written in 1969, this catchy but insubstantial song failed to appear on 'After

The Goldrush'. This version was recorded much later around the time of 'On The Beach'. It was a pleasant enough footnote to Young's career.

DEEP FORBIDDEN LAKE

Another country-influenced song with oblique, foreboding lyrics. Young felt that its inclusion was a pointer to a key moment in his career: "It hopefully signified the end of a long, dark period which started with 'Time Fades Away'".

LOVE IS A ROSE

This was the least noteworthy of the previously unreleased material on the compilation. In fact, it was little more than a rewrite of the melody of 'Dance, Dance, Dance'.

CAMPAIGNER

The last previously unheard track here was the most intriguing. Originally titled 'Requiem For A President', this had been written during the Stills/Young tour. Young had watched news footage of Nixon visiting his wife in hospital after she suffered a stroke. He was sufficiently moved to compose the sympathetic refrain "Even Richard Nixon has got soul". It showed that Young was capable of a more complex response to the former president's character than the anger voiced on 'Ohio'.

Full track listing: Down To The Wire; Burned; Mr Soul; Broken Arrow; Expecting To Fly; Sugar Mountain; I Am A Child; The Loner; The Old Laughing Lady; Cinnamon Girl; Down By The River; Cowgirl In The Sand; I Believe In You; After The Goldrush; Southern Man; Helpless; Ohio; Soldier; Old Man; A Man Needs A Maid; Harvest; Heart Of Gold; Star Of Bethlehem; The Needle And The Damage Done; Tonight's The Night; Tired Eyes; Walk On; For The Turnstiles; Winterlong; Deep Forbidden Lake; Like A Hurricane; Love Is A Rose; Cortez The Killer; Campaigner; Long May You Run.

Neil Young - Comes A Time

COMES A TIME

ORIGINAL RELEASE DATE: SEPTEMBER 1978

Predicting Young's next musical venture was never easy. During the summer of 1977 he began appearing in various bars in Santa Cruz with a pick-up group called The Ducks, which included former Moby Grape members Jeff Blackburn and Bob Moseley. That experiment was never captured on record and soon Young moved on, relocating to Nashville where he recorded this album with Nicolette Larson and the grandly named Gone With The Wind Orchestra. The release date was delayed for some time as a result of Young's dissatisfaction with the original pressing. Fortunately, the album was worth the delay. Unlike 'American Stars 'n Bars', it was a remarkably consistent work with a vitality and upfront production that was both impressive and beguiling. The artifice and over-elaborate arrangements that had spoiled parts of *Harvest* were absent here as Young used strings to subtle and unobtrusive effect. His singing had seldom, if ever, been better and Larson's harmonies proved the perfect foil. The playing was also faultless, with acoustic guitars used prominently for dramatic effect. Even the songs, which in such a context might have been overly sentimental, were never maudlin and occasionally veered into unexpected lyrical directions. Among the pastoral albums in the Young canon this is by far the most accomplished and impressive. Thanks to Larson's hit recording of 'Lotta Love' the album gained frequent FM airplay which gave Young his first US Top 20 record since 'Harvest'.

GOIN' BACK

Some memorable acoustic strumming opens the album on a strong note. Young's song of longing for all that has been lost is given a dramatic twist by the introduction of strings towards the end of the second verse. There is even a touch of apocalyptic imagery ("When fire fills the sky/These rocks... careering through space") amid the deceptively straightforward lyrics. What impresses most though is the excellent production, with careful consideration being given to the placement of each instrument.

COMES A TIME

The rapturous fiddle opening prefaces a striking duet between Young and Nicolette Larson which is engagingly tuneful when placed beside similar efforts on 'American Stars 'n Bars'. Again Young throws in some portentous imagery ("It's a wonder tall trees ain't laying down") to add depth to his reflections on the passage of time.

LOOK OUT FOR MY LOVE

Young's reunion with Crazy Horse proves the highlight of the entire album. The track opens with a strumming guitar that positively reverberates through the speakers. Young maximises the sense of drama and expectation by slowly introducing new elements into the song. As he sings "Was I hurt too bad?" Molina and Talbot enter for the first time on vocals, altering the mood significantly. Then, in one of his most inspired moves, Young decides to turn the tune electric mid-way through. The chunky rhythms of Crazy Horse add some musical onomatopoeia to the words "Hydraulic wipers pumping" as the track nears its climax. There's even some wah-wah guitar in the next verse to add to the variety on what is one of Young's best tracks from the

period. For those who believed that Crazy Horse could only be effective on long electric guitar workouts or bar room numbers then this was proof of how to use their talents in a more restrained musical context.

LOTTA LOVE

This song was originally intended for 'American Stars 'n Bars' until Young decided to allow Nicolette Larson to record a version first. She subsequently scored a US Top 10 hit with the composition. This version is equally commercial, with Crazy Horse providing the backing. Lyrically, it testifies to the insecurities implicit in new relationships, with the singer providing a veritable list of ideal requirements before acknowledging that the new love has yet to arrive.

PEACE OF MIND

More emotional self-questioning, with some powerful harmony work from Larson. Steel guitar and strings combine uneasily in the second verse against a backdrop of military-style drumming.

HUMAN HIGHWAY

Originally the title track for CSN&Y's great lost second studio album, this was an audience favourite at the time. In concert Young would occasionally change the lyrics to amusing effect. The banjo accompaniment suits the country arrangement, although it still seems strange that such an average song should have been considered as the title track to a CSN&Y record.

ALREADY ONE

Young takes a poignantly analytical look at a changing relationship, seemingly lost but not forgotten. The song has strong autobiographical overtones, reflecting on Young's separation from Carrie Snodgress and the child whose presence ensures that they remain in contact ("But we're already one/Our little son won't let us forget").

FIELD OF OPPORTUNITY

Young performs a country hoe-down backed by a Rufus Thibodeaux on fiddle. The song includes some amusing cod philosophical couplets – "I just don't have any answers my friend/Just this pile of old questions". Reviewers paid particular attention to the lines "In the field of opportunity, it's ploughing time again", equating its sentiments with Young's decision to record his most commercial album since *Harvest*.

MOTORCYCLE MAMA

For most listeners this was the album's fly in the ointment and one of Young's least loved tracks. Switching styles, he indulges himself in an irritating blues made worse by fuzz guitar and a keening Larson at her most vocally unattractive. The song subverts the album to such a degree that it comes close to destroying the entire mood of the second side. It almost seems like one of Young's perverse jokes.

FOUR STRONG WINDS

Young closes the album with Ian Tyson's folk chestnut from 1963. On one level it's an appropriate song for Young to cover with its allusions to Canada but, unlike the remainder of the album, the middle of the road arrangement sounds a little cloying, especially after you've been through the rigours of 'Time Fades Away' and 'Tonight's The Night'. The song brought Young some minor hit success in the UK, albeit at number 57.

NEIL YOUNG & CRAZY HORSE

RUST NEVER SLEEPS

RUST NEVER SLEEPS

ORIGINAL RELEASE DATE: JUNE 1979

While working on another experimental film, the "nuclear comedy" *Human Highway*, Young became intrigued by the quirky art-rock group Devo. He asked them to appear in the movie and they were filmed at the San Francisco punk club Mabuhay Gardens singing a mock version of 'After The Goldrush' and the first draft of a new Young song 'Hey Hey, My My (Into The Black).' While viewing the rushes for the film Young noticed that they were repeatedly using the phrase "rust never sleeps". The adage so appealed to Young that he decided to borrow it for the title of his next film and album. "I can relate to 'Rust Never Sleeps'," he claimed. "It relates to my career; the longer I keep on going the more I have to fight this corrosion. And now that's gotten to be like the World Series for me. The competition's there, whether I will corrode and eventually not be able to move anymore and just repeat myself until further notice or whether I will be able to expand and keep the corrosion down a little".

In order to "keep the corrosion down", Young re-enlisted Crazy Horse for a major tour and album. The latter was a masterstroke by Young, featuring several of the best songs he had written in recent years, divided into acoustic and electric sides. This idea had already been attempted in somewhat hamfisted fashion on 'American Stars 'n Bars' but this time he had the songs, the arrangements and a more coherent vision. The work elevated Young's artistic reputation to a new high, even encouraging favourable comparisons with Dylan who was also in the news at the time. As the decade wound to a close Young seemed on the cusp of a creative flow that would maintain his ascendancy throughout the Eighties. Few could have guessed what would happen next.

MY MY, HEY HEY
(OUT OF THE BLUE)

Recorded live in concert, this acoustic version was co-credited to Jeff Blackburn, a former member of Moby Grape, with whom Young had played in The Ducks. Contemporaneous critics complained about Young's glorification of Johnny Rotten, perhaps missing the point that it was really "rock'n'roll" itself that was being celebrated. The suggestion that it was "better to burn out" also brought accusations from some quarters that Young was glorifying suicide. In a macabre twist, those criticisms returned to haunt Young after the death of Kurt Cobain, whose suicide letter quoted lines from this song.

THRASHER

With acoustic guitar and harmonica, Young adopts the role of a folk troubadour in this fascinating narrative. The song begins with speculations on the effects of mechanisation on a farming community, then moves on to analyse Young's own position in the rock community. There's even a pun on artistes losing themselves in rock formations which sounds like a dig at CSN&Y's supergroup dreams. By the end of the song Young recognises his own place in the scheme of things and promises to surrender his career to this grim reaper at the appropriate moment.

RIDE MY LLAMA

This song sounds as though it was one of the

tracks intended for what Young called his "time travel" album. The fantasy meeting with a "man from Mars" means that the narrator now has the opportunity to journey wherever he wishes and can even transport a llama to his former neighbourhood. Mid-way through the song you can hear the audience clapping and there remains the unstated but likely conclusion that the substance the alien proffers for recreational use is good old-fashioned marijuana.

POCAHONTAS

This is one of Young's most accomplished acoustic tracks from the period and a perfect example of his ability to mix pathos and comedy. In describing the white man's merciless massacre of an Indian tribe, Young catalogues the tragedy with remarkable restraint. The line "They killed us in our tepee" places him in the centre of the action, but in the next instant he detaches himself from the scene. There is now a strangely impartial tone best exemplified by the word "might" in the lines: "They *might* have left some babies/Cryin' on the ground". Even while relating the horrific scene in the first person Young simultaneously seeks an academic's disinterested viewpoint and complicates the listener's response in the process. Are we to feel some relief that the soldiers showed crumbs of mercy in not killing all the babies? Or do we feel even greater indignation at the thought of the young left defenceless and possibly doomed to a slow death on open ground? Young's use of a qualifier such as "might" merely adds to the horror of the incident which gains even greater emotional force by the almost casual way in which he sings the verse. He then switches time periods, placing the narrator in the present day, living in a box room "with my Indian rug and a pipe to share". In the final verse there is the fantasy meeting between Young the narrator, Pocahontas and Marlon Brando which entranced and amused audiences when they first heard the lines in concert.

SAIL AWAY

Young neatly fuses the themes of the previous track in the opening two lines of this song: "I could live inside a tepee/I could die in Penthouse thirty-five". What follows is a fatalistic acceptance of whatever life offers, in common with the conclusion of 'Thrasher'. Thematically, you can't complain about the inclusion of 'Sail Away' although musically it sounds a little out of place, using the Nicolette Larson vocal harmonies from the 'Comes A Time' period.

POWDERFINGER

Another of Young's great narrative songs, this is almost cinematic in execution. It tells of a 22-year-old's moment of destiny when he is called upon to take decisive action against a marauding boat, an action that ends with his death. His dying wish is enshrined in a moving epitaph: "Just think of me as one you never figured/ Would fade away so young/With so much left undone/Remember me to my love, I know I'll miss her". Crazy Horse provide the ideal backing, allowing Young to invest the song with epic significance.

WELFARE MOTHERS

A simple construction and the perfect vehicle to allow Crazy Horse to rock out and enjoy themselves. The lyrics cleverly disguise lust as pseudo-social commentary with Young proclaiming the erotic benefits of mothers forced on welfare.

SEDAN DELIVERY

"Speedfreak rock" seems the most suitable description for this song, which moves from a discussion about a pool hall game with a woman troubled by varicose veins to a bigamist visiting a dentist and a drug dealer making a delivery to a mad scientist. The musical backdrop features Crazy Horse changing rhythm from fast to slow as if to comment on the lyrical confusion. This is Young looking back to the surreal spirit of mid-Sixties Dylan.

HEY HEY, MY MY
(INTO THE BLACK)

Amazingly, Jeff Blackburn does not receive a co-writing credit for this song, even though the melody and most of the words are the same as 'My My, Hey Hey (Out Of The Blue)'. The only real difference is the dramatic shift to electric with Young's feedback-drenched guitar burning the song into the audience's consciousness. He also plays a clever trick by asking the teasing question: "Is this the story of the Johnny Rotten?" Strangely enough none of the album's reviewers picked up on this key line which of course puts Young's point of view about the subject matter in some doubt.

LIVE RUST

ORIGINAL RELEASE DATE: JUNE 1979

Released less than a year after 'Rust Never Sleeps', this double live album consisted largely of Young and Crazy Horse's show at the Cow Palace, San Francisco on 22 October 1978. The show was filmed for inclusion in the film *Rust Never Sleeps*, effectively making this a soundtrack album as well as a memento of his winter tour. Throughout that series of concerts Young had employed strong visual effects to add a touch of theatre to the proceedings. Giant props were used to convey the idea of a child awakening into a nursery world of rock'n'roll. Meanwhile, roadies (nicknamed "road-eyes") would scurry across the stage dressed in cowls lit with burning eyes like the Jawas in the movie *Star Wars*. The shows, and later the film, met a mixed response from the critics, with at least one complaining that the theatrics belittled Young's artistry.

Originally, Young had intended to title this soundtrack album 'Rust Never Sleeps', seemingly oblivious to the confusion this would cause with the studio album of the same name. Viewed as a live album, this double proved a major disappointment. There was not one new song among its titles and large chunks of the work consisted of tracks already heard in a more pleasing studio context less than 12 months before. Had the album not been released so close to its predecessor or featured more varied material, it might have been more palatable. As it was, it left Young open to accusations of exploitation and unnecessary recycling. For a performer whose gigs over the last few years had produced such a wealth of unreleased and fascinatingly arranged material, this was a frustratingly lost opportunity to provide a live album of real originality.

Full track listing: Sugar Mountain; I Am A Child; Comes A Time; After The Goldrush; My My, Hey Hey (Out Of The Blue); When You Dance I Can Really Love; The Loner; The Needle And The Damage Done; Lotta Love; Sedan Delivery; Powderfinger; Cortez The Killer; Cinnamon Girl; Like A Hurricane; Hey Hey, My My (Into The Black); Tonight's The Night.

NEIL YOUNG   HAWKS & DOVES

HAWKS & DOVES

ORIGINAL RELEASE DATE: OCTOBER 1980

Young's first appearance on record during the Eighties was an inauspicious contribution to the film soundtrack 'Where The Buffalo Roam' on which he could be heard performing mainly instrumental versions of 'Home On The Range'. Towards the end of the year the often underrated 'Hawks & Doves' was released which, in common with 'Rust Never Sleeps' and 'American Stars 'n Bars', was consciously divided into two stylistically contrasting sides. The acoustic side was excellent and featured several enigmatic but affecting ballads, some reaching back to the early/mid-Seventies. At times, Young appeared to be burying his feelings in a frequently unfathomable personal symbolism which was nevertheless intriguing. If the lyrics on the acoustic half suggested that he was toying with his listener, then the country segment was pure wilfulness. By the end of the album he emerged as a bloodied patriot with a sardonic smile on his face. The clumsy political satire seemed transparent given the vocal phrasing and hackneyed arrangements of the country tunes but, following his pro-Reagan statements later in the decade, it became difficult to decide where the joke began and ended. In the event it mattered little for the album failed to sell well. Its schizoid construction and contrasting tones puzzled listeners, while the lack of a tour or any promotion meant that it failed to reach the mass audience that greeted 'Rust Never Sleeps'. Young was beginning his slide back into cultdom.

LITTLE WING

The reflective, acoustic side of the album opens with this charming mood piece. Taken literally, the song could be about a migrating bird or, alternatively, an Indian girl or idealised maternal figure. The lines "She leaves her feathers as they fall" recall a similar allusion from 'Birds': "feathers fall around you". Six months before the album's release David Crosby told me that Young had offered him 'Little Wing' for his forthcoming solo album. It seems that Young eventually decided to revive the song himself, having written it back in 1975.

THE OLD HOMESTEAD

Arguably the highlight of the album, this remains one of Young's most fascinating and oblique compositions. I have always suspected that the song was an allegory about the turbulent history of CSN&Y and although later commentators have repeated my views, Young has remained tight-lipped on the matter. Any allegorical interpretation rests on the identification of the three birds as CS&N, Young as the Rider, and Crazy Horse playing themselves. In this scenario, I have always assumed that the Rider who demands "Why do you ride that Crazy Horse?" is manager Elliot Roberts, although at this point any further analysis is purely speculative. Young provides few clues to help unravel the allegory, much of which remains hidden. Not that you need an explanation to appreciate the song which is one of Young's best and most sorely neglected. It comes as no surprise to learn that he composed this in 1974. Both the mood and the enigmatic lyrics recall the better

moments of 'On The Beach'. Here, Tom Scribner adds to the eerie feel of the song by wobbling a saw at key moments. The whole effect is quite fascinating.

LOST IN SPACE

A tale of a lost love is trapped somewhere in this composition, but you have to wade through Young's reflections on underwater civilisations and similarly obscure matters to follow the narration. At one point, he plays the comedian by introducing the "Marine Munchkin" to sing a tribute to the ocean floor, as though he's writing a subaquatic *Wizard Of Oz*. Listeners intrigued by the lyrics are likely to emerge asking such questions as: "Who is the queen? What's the significance of the magic pen? Is the infinity board a reference to God's creation?" More than any other album in the Young canon, this presents more questions than answers.

CAPTAIN KENNEDY

The opening of this song is strikingly reminiscent of Stills' 'Know You Got To Run', a track which was of course segued into Young's 'Everybody I Love You'. Here, Young tells the story of a young mariner, re-enacting his father's career and betraying similar fears to the hero of 'Powderfinger' about the consequences of war. The pertinent use of the name Kennedy may be a red herring, although it should be remembered that JFK served in the navy during the Second World War.

STAYIN' POWER

The country side of the album commences with this simple statement of the need for true grit in order to surmount life's vicissitudes. The fiddle of Rufus Thibodeaux dominates, driving the song along like a rallying call to the nation's unheralded hard-working lovers.

COASTLINE

This thinly-disguised tribute to Young's wife is again expressed as a hearty C&W celebration. At the time, few outside his immediate circle knew that he was devoting much of his life to looking after his disabled son. With hindsight, this song can be seen as a rousing affirmation of his new work ethic. Yet there is a wonderfully bathetic comic moment at the close of the chorus when he congratulates himself and his wife for rising punctually: "High on the

mountain tops above the clouds/No wonder we get a little loud/We don't back down from no trouble/We do get up in the morning".

UNION MAN

This light satire was directed against the American Federation of Musicians. Young portrays a staunch union man attending the weekly meeting and presents the main subject under discussion: a vote pertaining to the issue "Live music is better, bumper stickers should be issued". Everyone in attendance whoops "ay" and, not surprisingly, there are no dissenters.

COMIN' APART AT EVERY NAIL

Young's latest female backing singer Ann Hillary O'Brien is the key figure whose soaring harmonies blast out the chorus of this song. Young, meanwhile, crows along in his most affected "Nashville voice" proclaiming the rights of the working man, caught between the government and the mob. The patriotism is expressed in an ambivalent air, with the need for vigilance seemingly uppermost in Young's mind.

HAWKS & DOVES

Young's political satire reaches new heights of painful comedy here. In light of his reactionary comments later in the decade, some commentators have tended to take the sentiments of this song seriously, as if it was unambiguously jingoistic. Yet it's difficult to take the viewpoints seriously when Young sings the tune in such an affected voice. Indeed, it seems that he's enjoying some method acting, placing himself in the role of a boorish, inarticulate flag waver. His political philosophy is summed up in the memorably stumbling couplet: "I ain't tongue tied, just don't got nothing to say/I'm proud to be livin' in the USA".

RE-AC-TOR

ORIGINAL RELEASE DATE: OCTOBER 1981

Young reunited with Crazy Horse for this album but failed to reach the creative heights of earlier collaborations. By his own admission, he was severely distracted by having to look after his younger son who was undergoing physiological therapy for cerebral palsy. As Young noted: "The songs I'm writing during the programme we're doing indicate to me how much what I'm doing every day is the strongest single influence on my work... driving, implacable, repetitive." The album reflects Young's physical and emotional state, at times betraying a mechanistic feel as though it was made by an automaton. Human emotion seems virtually drained from the songs and Crazy Horse appear unsure and unable to pick up on the usual feel of a Young session. Instead, they just bang away as if waiting for him to spark something new. But Young is clearly keeping his feelings, emotions and opinions at bay. The lyrics seem like they were inspired by reading a car manual. This is Young with the emotional shutters locked tight.

OPERA STAR

The opening track is a basic riff supplemented by some less than wry reflections on the unsophisticated lifestyle of the average rock star. The Santa Claus chorus ("Ho ho ho ho ho ho") sounds like Crazy Horse are poking fun at the whole idea, which is understandable.

SURFER JOE AND MOE THE SLEAZE

Crazy Horse's unconvincing backing vocals are even more irksome here as Young offers a day at the beach ("Plenty of women, plenty of booze"). There's a half-decent riff that momentarily attracts attention, but you get the impression that Young's heart isn't in the song. Such a view is partly confirmed by guitarist Frank Sampedro: "A lot of the tracks didn't groove all the way through, like 'Surfer Joe'. The groove would slow down, then speed up. So, instead of trying to re-cut them, we would spend all our time hitting everything we could find to fill the holes in the song – banging tambourines, pieces of metal, standing around doing hand claps. We didn't understand why we were doing this. But we also didn't understand how distracted Neil was. He just wanted to get through it".

T-BONE

Young takes his search for minimalism to fresh extremes with this song which simply consists of the words "Got mashed potatoes/Ain't got no T-Bone" endlessly repeated. It certainly wasn't going to get him any songwriting awards and the accompanying guitar work was equally nondescript. This was simply Young attempting to have fun by playing lazily without a care for his audience's reaction. As he explained: "The night we recorded that we didn't have anything else happening in particular. We were just in the studio and we had already recorded the songs that we thought we were going to be recording and we really felt like playing. So I just went in, picked up the guitar and started playing and, if you notice, the song starts with a straight cut through the middle. We'd already started playing before the machine started. So that was a one-shot deal. I just made up the lyrics and we did the whole thing that night. It was a one-take thing. It seems like the lyrics were just on my mind. It's very repetitive

but I'm not such an inventive guy. I thought those two lines were good. Every time, it sounded a bit different to me when I started singing. Then I was thinking about something else. I really like that cut better than the rest on 'Re-ac-tor'."

GET BACK ON IT

More basic R&B, this time with a honky tonk piano thrown in and some infuriatingly Neanderthal backing vocals. Young name drops General Custer and Robert E. Lee for no apparent reason beyond the fact that they're dead and he isn't.

SOUTHERN PACIFIC

Although far from startling, this at least sounded like a half-decent train song – a sort of Casey Jones entering retirement with only his pension and memories to look forward to. There's a neat growling burst of guitar just as the song reaches its close. With little to choose from, Reprise twice released this as a single, with different B-sides.

MOTOR CITY

Although inspired by Detroit and performed in the R&B vein of the other songs, the arrangement was obviously country-influenced. Young takes a cheap shot at Japanese cars and reminisces about his Army jeep, but the lyrics and melody are banal beyond belief.

RAPID TRANSIT

Here he plays around with a simple riff, stutters some words and makes gargling noises as he sings. The song threatens to get going with a guitar solo but soon fizzles out. At least the childish vocal tricks are worth a laugh, briefly calling to mind Daltrey's famous stutter on The Who's 'My Generation'.

SHOTS

In many respects the faltering reputation of the album was saved almost single-handedly by this seven-and-a-half minute closing track. Although the credits copyright the song as 1981, Young's keener fans of the period will have been familiar with the composition from as early as 1978, when it was performed at the Boarding House. Back then, it was a thoughtful delicate ballad with a sparse arrangement. Here, it is completely transformed, perhaps like no Young song before or since. Crazy Horse provide a gut-wrenching backing with guitars playing like scatter guns across the speakers. The ending is an explosive battlefield of feedback, which leaves the listener wondering why Young had not invested some of the same passion across the remainder of this frustrating record.

TRANS

ORIGINAL RELEASE DATE: JANUARY 1983

Young's first release for his new label Geffen saw him under the spell of electro pop, with more than a passing nod to the German group Kraftwerk. He had recently toured extensively with the Trans Band, featuring Nils Lofgren, Ben Keith, Ralph Molina, Joe Lala and, most surprisingly, Bruce Palmer, whom he had last seen during the Springfield days. Computer technology was Young's new hobby-horse with the vocoder literally transforming his voice into an otherworldly dissonance. As Young explained: "I spend most of the time trying to remain open to new things. They reflect the fact that I've got so interested in electronics and machines. I feel that with the new digital and computerised equipment I can get my hands on now, I can do things I could never do before." The album was an interesting diversion but failed to fulfil its own convictions and was fatally compromised by mixing radical futuristic songs with a handful of ballads borrowed from an earlier project. It would have been a bolder, more genuinely experimental work if Young had maintained the courage to use the vocoder and synths on every track rather than diluting the album. As it was, he hit the mark perfectly on a couple of songs but lacked enough quality material to produce a genuinely thrilling work.

LITTLE THING CALLED LOVE

The album begins deceptively with one of Young's more commercial offerings, sung in a clear, on-key voice. Pleasing but superficial, the song sounds like a sweetener before the more adventurous work that follows. It's as if Young has deliberately sequenced the album to ensure that the first track is not too intimidating. It comes as no surprise to learn that this song, and the similarly incongruous 'Hold On To Your Love', were taken from the aborted sessions of an earlier unreleased album for Geffen.

COMPUTER AGE

Enter the vocoder, allied to a strong upbeat melody. The lyrics conjure up a vision of a frantic, highly mechanised world in which it seems difficult to distinguish the robotic from the organic: "Precious metal lines/Molded into highways/ Running through me/So microscopically". In visualising the song for a possible video, Young took the concept further: "There's 'Computer Age' which had to do with the doctors in the hospital talking to one another. There are families trying to get to the hospital, getting caught in traffic and watching the lights change. Their eyes start to be like traffic lights."

WE R IN CONTROL

Here Young takes a leaf from Devo's book, using repeated slogans to present a dystopian vision of machines taking over society. "It's sung by the airport and traffic systems," he explained. The track suggests that Young had a distinct dramatic structure in mind when he composed several of these songs.

TRANSFORMER MAN

In contrast to 'We R In Control', this celebrates the liberating aspects of technology. The song was inspired by the equipment which helped his handicapped younger son to communicate with the outside world. In Young's imaginary scenario, "The nurses sing to the little kid: 'Control the action/Push of a button/Trying to break through/There's so much to do/We haven't made it yet'. They're telling the kid that he's got to press the button or he's not going to be able to communicate. That was the beginning of my ideas of my son being able to communicate through technology." The song has greater emotional force if you forget Young's explanation and approach the lyrics as the songwriter's own reaction to the transformed boy. Either way, it's one of the best tracks on the album, combining Young's normal vocal with vocoded replies.

COMPUTER COWBOY
(AKA SYSCRUSHER)

The most humorous track on the album sees Young attempting a 21st century country 'n' western tune. Computerised clip clops imitate the sound of a horse while the cowboy, a sort of techno Frankie Laine, updates an old tune by singing "Come a ky ky yippee yi yippee yi ay". The subtitle 'Syscrusher' is shorthand for "system crusher", the cowboy's nocturnal alter ego. As Young enthusiastically explained at the time: "During the day he was a cowboy. All his cows were the same; they were digital cows, square block cows. He had a floodlight out on the pasture which he kept lit all night, so there were 24 hours of light for the cows to be eating and moving towards their final goal. The perfect cattle ranch. But at night when he turned on the lights, he'd go into the city and start fucking around with the computers of those companies. He'd go inside buildings, fuck up the memory systems and the government records."

HOLD ON TO YOUR LOVE

In the midst of the computerised drama, Young inserts a standard love song in his human voice. Elsewhere, this would be just another minor Young ballad, but here it sounds completely out of place, serving mainly to open the second side of the album on a safe and timid note.

SAMPLE AND HOLD

With such a distinctive riff, it is not that surprising that this was later issued as a 12-inch single and even suffered a disco mix. It's probably the highlight of the album, featuring some great vocoder interplay between Young and Lofgren. The lyrics are also fascinating, alluding to what seems to be a robotic dating service.

MR SOUL

The surprise revival of Buffalo Springfield's minor hit probably came as a shock to some old fans but it was typical of Young's mischievous humour. Again it's sung in his normal voice with the vocoder (possibly featuring Lofgren) coming in at the end of the second verse. A strange and not entirely welcome synthesis of the old and the new.

LIKE AN INCA

On paper, this lengthy closing track seemed likely to be the high point of the album, serving a similar function to 'Shots' on 'Re-ac-tor'. The title placed it in the great tradition of 'Cortez The Killer' but there the similarity ends. The song combines several of Young's favourite themes: idealised Aztec civilisations, the threat of nuclear oblivion, the 'After The Goldrush' vision of escaping the bomb. Unfortunately, what looks so promising on the lyric sheet is spoiled by a frankly boring arrangement in which Young rigidly sticks to a synth groove. Having championed the new technology throughout much of the album, Young closes the experiment on an anti-climactic note leaving the listener gasping to hear an extended guitar solo in the grand tradition of Crazy Horse.

Neil Young

NEIL and the SHOCKING PINKS

Everybody's Rockin'

EVERYBODY'S ROCKIN'

ORIGINAL RELEASE DATE: AUGUST 1983

The genre switching relentlessly continued, with Young now going full circle from futuristic electro popster to Fifties-styled rockabilly singer. On the sleeve he was pictured in a pink jacket with greased back hair. If the sleeve was amusing the musical contents were no joke. At a scandalous 24 minutes in length the album seemed over before it began. This would not have mattered if the material had been of consistently excellent quality, but the majority of the songs were throwaway items. Perversely, Young championed the album but later admitted that its conception was mainly to upset his record company, whose president David Geffen had dared question his musical direction. In the end it was the album's purchasers who suffered more than Geffen who quickly wrote it off. At least the record gained some life when it was played as a segment in concert.

BETTY LOU'S GOT A BRAND NEW PAIR OF SHOES

Young attempts to kick-start his rockabilly album with this Bobby Freeman composition. Beyond a burst of rock'n'roll piano and Ben "King" Keith letting go on alto sax there's not too much to recommend.

RAININ' IN MY HEART

Not the Buddy Holly classic but a James Moore/Jerry West composition, featuring Young on piano and harmonica. The Fats Domino influence is noticeable while the spoken part is so unconvincing that it sounds nothing less than a parody in Bonzo Dog Doo-Dah Band vein.

PAYOLA BLUES

At 3 minutes 8 seconds, this was the longest cut on the album, and also the best. Young dedicates the song to that fallen and long dead Fifties' disc jockey, Alan Freed. Comparing past payola with contemporary hyping tactics Young sings: "The things they do today will make a saint out of you". Although the record was played on air and most found it very amusing, Young felt that it might just have ruffled a few over-sensitive programmers. "I guess there was a little flak," he conceded to *Musician*. "It was kind of an embarrassment to some people. But it was all in good fun. That's the way it is anyway, everybody knows that. It's all about money, the whole thing. Anybody who thinks it isn't is kidding themselves and everybody else. Because what goes on in parking lots is nobody's business but those people who are there and, believe me, they're out there. This is still America. I know what payola is and there are different kinds of payola; there is payola where the artiste puts his money into it, and there is payola where the record company puts their money into it... It's no secret and it's part of the mechanism of things. That's how Mr Big stays Mr Big. That's why the little guy with the little independent label has got to have something great to break through to where the people will say, 'I want to hear that record! I don't care whether they pay you'. "

WONDERIN'

In early 1970 Young played this in concert as one of his hokey, country tunes. Its unexpected

appearance here as a doo-wop influenced excursion underlines the point that few Young songs can be confidently consigned to unreleased oblivion with complete assurance. Although not of great import, the song was catchy enough to be plucked from the heap and issued as a single, complete with a promotional video.

KINDA FONDA WANDA

This song gives Young the opportunity to name drop a host of famous song titles from the annals of Fifties/Sixties pop: Ricky Nelson's 'Hello Mary Lou', Buddy Holly's 'Peggy Sue', Ritchie Valens' 'Donna' and, most funnily, Dion's 'Runaround Sue' (who is accused of "screwing around", unlike Fonda Wanda). The song is an ephemerally amusing pastiche but does not bear repeated listening, while the attempt at Jerry Lee Lewis's piano style is appalling.

JELLYROLL MAN

Just under two minutes long, this is another superficial piece of ersatz rockabilly, with Young attempting to impress us with a short harmonica solo.

BRIGHT LIGHTS, BIG CITY

Quite simply one of the worst covers of Jimmy Reed's classic that I've ever heard. A big mistake.

CRY, CRY, CRY

Composed by Young, this is at least a bit more exuberant and the guitar parts are reasonable. The main problem is that he's not accomplished enough as a vocalist to front the doo-wop chorus in the background.

MYSTERY TRAIN

It sounds like sacrilege, but could have been a lot worse. Young does his best but succeeds only in reminding us how marvellous Elvis Presley's phrasing was at the time he recorded this classic for Sun. The Canadian attempts to invest the song with a few vocal embellishments but ultimately resembles an Elvis pub singer. His fellow players fare no better. The instrumental breaks lack any vestige of the verve or mystery that Scotty and Bill brought to the song. At least the backing singers realise the futility of emulating the original, and end the song by attempting to copy the sound of a train whistle.

EVERYBODY'S ROCKIN'

The title track offers a slight end to an even slighter album. The closing notes feature a laughing sax, an appropriate comment as it turns out. If only Young had released this album as an EP he would have saved us all a lot of money and saved himself from the continued critical castigation surrounding this 24-minute piece of camp ephemera.

OLD WAYS

ORIGINAL RELEASE DATE: AUGUST 1985

A lthough Young's foray into Nashville-style country music seemed the latest in his series of genre experiments, it was more serious and long-lasting than other recent ventures. Young later suggested that this was partly due to his lengthy dispute with Geffen Records, who were still reluctant to issue his more arcane work and had already rejected an early version of 'Old Ways'. Indeed, they were on the brink of suing the performer on the ludicrous charge of delivering material which they deemed "uncharacteristic of Neil Young". It seems to have escaped their notice that Young had been doing this, on and off, since 'Time Fades Away'. Rather than capitulate to their demand for more commercial product, he dug in his heels. As Young argued: "I told them the longer you sue me for playing country music, the longer I'm going to play country music. Either you back off or I'm going to play country music for ever."

At the time, Young was as good as his word and took to the road with the International Harvesters for the best part of two years. Nor were his reasons for playing country purely to irk Geffen. He found a sense of community in country music that appealed to him as he reached middle-age. As he explained to *Melody Maker*: "I see country music, I see people who take care of their own. You've got 75-year-old guys on the road. That's what I was put here to do. So I want to make sure I surround myself with people who are going to take care of me, because I'm in it for the long run." Indeed, from his comments at the time,

reinforced by those close to him, Young seemingly looked no further than country music for his future creative endeavours.

This album summed up the period well, displaying his immersion in the genre and introducing such country greats as Willie Nelson and Waylon Jennings to the Young song catalogue.

THE WAYWARD WIND

The album commences with what is probably Young's most successful cover song. His confident vocal is greatly enhanced by another female voice – this time Denise Draper. Terry McMillan's harmonica adds an eerie touch, but what really makes the song is the extraordinarily effective string arrangement by Chuck Cochran. The 17-piece orchestra provides an evocative backdrop, akin to a high-class film soundtrack on one of the best arranged songs of Young's career.

GET BACK TO THE COUNTRY

Not so much a song title, more a statement of intent. Again the accompaniment is impressive with Terry McMillan on Jew's harp, Rufus Thibodeaux on fiddle and Bobby Thompson on banjo. This is not a question of Young imitating a style but immersing himself in a genre with musicians familiar with its traditions. Waylon Jennings' vocal support, more intrusive elsewhere, also fits in perfectly here.

ARE THERE ANY MORE REAL COWBOYS?

Young's lament for the real cowboy of times past is another impressive song. This time Willie Nelson takes a verse and also appears on acoustic guitar. The effect is to step beyond fickle genre experimentation and appreciate the form without the stigma of pastiche.

ONCE AN ANGEL

This over-sentimental affirmation of family values is a pleasant enough ballad in its own right, but gains additional power from the wealth of backing vocalists employed to sweeten the track. Interestingly, the line-up is all female: Doana Cooper, Gail Davies, Betsy Hammer, Pam Rose, Janis Oliver-Gill, Mary Ann Kennedy, Kristine Oliver-Arnold and Leona Williams. Having previously employed Nicolette Larson, Linda Ronstadt and Emmylou Harris for such backing, Young this time prefers a cast of thousands.

MISFITS

The highlight of the album and the maverick tune in the pack is this triptych tale of a space station crew watching Muhammed Ali videos, a prostitute in a hotel lobby and a figure riding the highway. The strings sweep dramatically across the track reinforcing an enigma that is never resolved, while Joe Allen's upright bass maintains the rhythm. At peak moments the song moves into a melody line highly reminiscent of Gene Pitney's '24 Hours From Tulsa', while Doana Cooper adds a shivering backing vocal and Terry McMillan slips in a harmonica lilt. The overall effect is mesmeric and proof positive that Young, even in the context of a seemingly straight country album, can add a touch of mystery. This remains a serious candidate for the best Young song of the decade.

CALIFORNIA SUNSET

A relaxing tune after the drama of 'Misfits' with the fiddle of Rufus Thibodeaux in strong evidence. There is also the eminent composer Spooner Oldham on piano. This live performance ends with a respectful response from the audience.

OLD WAYS

Waylon Jennings provides backing vocals on this song in which Young warns: "Old ways can be a ball and chain". Those words could stand as an axiom that he has always followed. As the album reaches its final stages, it's noticeable how the songs appear to lose much of their grandeur, as if Young is content to wallow in traditional country themes without adding his distinctive mark to the material.

MY BOY

A quaint and syrupy ballad in which Young muses over the speed with which his eldest son is growing up. Thematically, it can be seen as a belated follow-up to 'Already One', and comes close to

mawkishness. For once on this album, Young dominates the song musically, playing banjo, harmonica and electric guitar.

BOUND FOR GLORY

Young and Jennings combine, with Waylon singing an entire verse solo. It's typical Nashville material, featuring a wayward husband living on the edge and threatening to leave his wife and kids. Surprisingly, Young claimed it was his favourite track on the album at the time, explaining, "I wrote that one on a word processor in the back of my bus while I was rolling. I wrote it with a couple of beers and a little smoke. The bus was rolling down the road and I typed it out and I knew the melody in my head already."

WHERE IS THE HIGHWAY TONIGHT?

The album closes with another duet with Waylon Jennings. Again, Young fully immerses himself in the genre, perhaps a little too much so for parts of his rock audience. What is most noticeable about the album is that the earlier orchestrated songs sound far superior to the straight country songs towards the close of the work. The opposite was largely the case on 'Harvest'.

Neil Young
LANDING ON WATER

LANDING ON WATER

ORIGINAL RELEASE DATE: JULY 1986

Along with 'Everybody's Rockin'' this represented the nadir of Young's recording career. With the assistance of bassist Danny Kortchmar, drummer Steve Jordan and several synthesisers, he recorded an album of songs completely lacking in distinction, with dull arrangements, banal lyrics and questionable tunes buried beneath irritating percussion. The extent to which Young had lost a grip on his musical career was summed up in his comments to *Rolling Stone* where he said of the album: "I was finding my rock'n'roll roots again and my vibrancy as a musician. Something came alive; it was like a bear waking up." In truth, it sounded like a bear slowly being bludgeoned to death. In keeping with the music, the sleeve artwork was the worst of Young's career.

WEIGHT OF THE WORLD

Synth drums are prominent in this opening track in which the narrator portrays himself as a shy, troubled introvert transformed upon meeting an idealised woman. The repetitive, unrelenting synth backing ultimately levels the song to tiresome inanity.

VIOLENT SIDE

This is better, if for no other reason than the presence of the San Francisco Boys' Chorus. Here at least the synths provide an appropriate backing to Young's mantra-like commands to "control the violent side". There is a paranoid aspect to the composition, a feature that will be repeated later on the album. Young's passion bursts through towards the end of the song as he's engulfed by the full wave of the boy chorus.

HIPPIE DREAM

The most powerful and provocative track on the album begins, suitably enough, with the refrain of 'Tired Eyes' – "Please take my advice". But even as he completes those words Young adds "Don't listen to me" as though he is unsure about the sagacity of his warnings. Feelings of paranoia are again present as the narrator warns: "Don't bat an eye/Don't waste a word/Don't mention nothin'/That could go unheard". The allusion to Crosby's 'Wooden Ships' fantasy is pertinent enough in the first verse and far more critical than Jackson Brown was in his reply song 'For Everyman'. By the end of song though, Young goes further by pointing the finger explicitly at Crosby: "Another flower child gone to seed/In an ether-filled room of meat hooks/It's so ugly". For anyone who regularly saw Crosby on the pipe, this is powerful stuff. As Young confirmed: "I wrote that one for Crosby. But I guess it could have been for me, or for anybody. It's really about the excesses of our generation. From hippie to yuppie – it's been quite an evolution."

BAD NEWS BEAT

A blandly executed song about a guy who loses his love and considers contacting her again, while the incessant backing tolls the "bad news beat".

TOUCH THE NIGHT

This track opens with one of the most clichéd heavy metal riffs imaginable. Musically, it only

improves slightly as images of urban destruction flash by. At one point Young threatens one of his extended guitar solos, but the result is flaccid and the song rapidly degenerates into another dull rhythm track.

PEOPLE ON THE STREET

More of the same from Young – urban imagery, deathly dull arrangements and an especially unattractive vocal intervention by Danny Kortchmar and Steve Jordan.

HARD LUCK STORIES

Lyrically, the unarresting theme concerns an irksome caller always complaining and bringing bad news. Young may as well have called it 'Bad News Beat, Part II'. The simple melody grows tiresome long before the song is over.

I GOT A PROBLEM

The hardest-sounding track on the album features heavy metal style guitar with the drums upfront. A catchy, though mindless, melody propels the composition and Young at least gets the opportunity to rock out a bit. Beyond that, it's completely unremarkable. If this is Young's idea of contemporary music in 1986 then you have to question his perspective and record collection.

PRESSURE

The almost laughable chorus is reminiscent of one of Ray Davies' rants against the everyday problems of life. Young laces his protests with an attack on MTV, pre-empting the title track of a future album.

DRIFTER

Another disarmingly simple synth backing over which Young sings about the need for personal freedom. It's as uninteresting and inane musically as it is lyrically. The track concludes with the equivalent of a synth jamming session during which Young uneasily throws in some lead guitar work which is insufficiently arresting to save the song.

NEIL YOUNG & CRAZY HORSE

LIFE

LIFE

ORIGINAL RELEASE DATE: JULY 1987

It was indicative of how low Young's stock had fallen that this average album was considered something of a creative comeback. The fact that he had reunited with Crazy Horse was greeted with much relief from die-hard fans but the musical results still left much to be desired. At least Young was back to writing some decent songs and singing well. Unfortunately, Crazy Horse would not be given an immediate opportunity to improve upon their efforts here. Having participated in the "Rusted Out Garage Tour" they joined Young on a European jaunt which was less than successful, with some venues failing to reach capacity. Relations between Young and his backing group were becoming increasingly strained. "I could feel it starting to slip away," Young recalled. "I never ever wanted to be in front of people and have them pay to see me when I'm not 100 per cent there... I may come back to Crazy Horse again some day, but it seems unlikely."

MIDEAST VACATION

The album starts impressively with Young's tale of a former Highway Patrolman and possible war veteran caught up in a Middle Eastern political nightmare. The tone is both sinister and satirical as the protagonist seeks Gadaffi, only to be intercepted by the CIA who tell him to "stop sniffing at smoking guns". In the mideastern town, he witnesses a demonstration in which the participants chant "Death to America", a view which transforms him into a fighting machine ("Rambo in the disco"). The black humour is a new slant for Young and a possible reaction to the criticism he was receiving in the liberal press for his pro-Reagan sentiments. In using a character to voice unfashionable views, Young could hide himself and laugh at the world at the same time. As he explained: "You can only do so much about yourself. It wears thin and becomes less valid the more there is. So I guess I evolved out of that to a great degree, though it's still part of my music."

LONG WALK HOME

Stacking the better songs at the start, Young again tackles a political theme, this time dealing with American foreign policy from Vietnam to Beirut. Young sees a world in which expediency is the common currency and alliances a mere moral convenience ("We balance the power from hour to hour"). In observing such cynicism, Young can only offer more questions: "Why do we feel the double-edged blade cutting through our hands?"

AROUND THE WORLD

A less impressive song than its predecessors sees Young simultaneously speculating on political upheavals ("Leaders fall, leaders rise") and changing fashions ("Fashions change, styles change"). Synths abound, sometimes creating a pseudo-raga effect. The vagueness of the song is perhaps explained by the circumstances of its composition. Young: "I wrote it in Daytona Beach when I was real sick with the flu – I had to cancel five dates. And I wrote that song when I woke up."

INCA QUEEN

A welcome return to the Aztec myths that occasionally fuel Young's imagination, this is an acoustic offering in marked contrast to 'Cortez The Killer'. Flutes and bird sounds are in evidence as Young relates a tale of idolatry in which an Inca Queen is worshipped. Her subjects attempt to build a city in the clouds which, she predicts, will bring a spaceship to take them away. It's a strange fusion of Aztec legend with a sci-fi 'After The Goldrush' scenario. At one point Young even introduces elephants into Peru in one of his more amusing geographical *faux pas*.

TOO LONELY

Young revisits The Rolling Stones' 'Satisfaction' riff while Molina plays uneasily along using a click track. All in all, it's one of the lesser tracks on the album with lyrics which vaguely equate wealth with lovelessness.

PRISONERS OF ROCK'N'ROLL

"We never listen to the record company man," Young boasts at the beginning of this song. It's a prosaic piece which would be absolutely redundant were it not for the underlying humour. Those aware of Young's problems with his record label could enjoy this as a playful put-down. Young and Crazy Horse categorise themselves as the prisoners with Geffen Records cast as jailers. The defiant cry "We don't want to be good" is Young's blunt reply to requests for more commercial product as he refuses to take "orders from record company clowns".

CRYIN' EYES

Already familiar to more diligent fans from Young's live performances with The Ducks, this is a less impressive, synth version of the hard-biting song. Although it sounds slightly neutered when taken out of its bar-room setting, it's still pleasing to hear the song on record.

WHEN YOUR LONELY HEART BREAKS

"Don't be crying for good times... don't sit counting your mistakes," sings Young to the lonely-hearted. His vocals sound sufficiently anguished, but the arrangement is singularly dull.

WE NEVER DANCED

An overdue reunion with producer/arranger Jack Nitzsche is the most interesting feature of this unusual closing track. The opaque lyrics, in which Young fantasises about a ballroom between heaven and earth, are set against recurring piano notes. The result is one of the slightly more interesting songs on the album but it is an experiment that remains undeveloped.

THIS NOTE'S FOR YOU

ORIGINAL RELEASE DATE: APRIL 1988

Although this album saw Young returning to the genre experiments of earlier in the decade, it also heralded his artistic rehabilitation. In the unlikely area of blues and power swing, Young found a vehicle for his art that actually worked. Significantly, the album coincided with Young's welcome return to Reprise Records. So why did this album work so successfully when other similarly experimental pieces failed? The probable answer is that Young was more focused and had learned to use the generic shifts to his own creative advantage. The arrangements here were all impressive and the integration of brass and Young's guitar work added depth to the songs. In concert The Blue Notes (renamed Ten Men Workin') proved the perfect foil for Young's new songs of urban unrest. Two of these, 'Sixty To Zero' and 'Ordinary People' were heavily influenced by mid-period Dylan and were rightly acclaimed by Young aficionados as among the most compelling material heard from him in years. Alas, the full live versions of these epics would remain unreleased, but this album is a stirring reminder of Young's surprise return to form after a barren and frustratingly erratic eight years.

TEN MEN WORKIN'

The sheer freshness of Young's performance here coupled with the crisp production confirm that his genre experimentation is at last about to pay major dividends. The brass section play upfront with Young interweaving key notes on guitar. As he recalled to Dave Zimmer: "I had this groove going through my head and I was playing it on my guitar, which is actually my wife's guitar, which she's had since she was just a little teenybopper... I'd be walking around the house playing. And I had this groove thing going, didn't have any lyrics, but I don't try and make up words... I never just try and think of something clever. So the way 'Ten Men Workin'' came to me was... one morning I was getting ready to go into where

we recorded the Blue Notes record, on
Melrose Avenue across from the Hollywood
Cemetery. One of the guys, the engineer of
my boat, had a Men At Work T-shirt on. I just
kept lookin' at that T-shirt and started thinking,
'Yeah, that's me, I'm working, and we're working.' It's like we were building or something.
We had this job to do. It was like it was our
mission to make people feel good and to
make them dance." The American single
release of this track included the otherwise
unavailable 'I'm Goin''.

THIS NOTE'S FOR YOU

Young's satire of corporate sponsorship was
a great crowd pleaser in concert that went on
to become a *cause célèbre* on video. MTV initially refused to screen Young's biting send-up
of famous television commercials, arguing that
he was guilty of "product placement". Within
a year, the station would nominate the offend-
ing item Best Video Of The Year while
Young's CD single featured an extra live version of the song. In attacking Pepsi, Coke,
Budweiser and Miller, Young was aware that
he could not completely escape from their per-
vasive influence. As he pointed out: "That's

kind of idealistic because when you get right
down to it I have to play the Budweiser concert series because they make a deal with the
promoter. I can't get around it, but I want people to know that it's not me making the deal
with Budweiser and Miller. They bought all the
places where I play."

COUPE DE VILLE

Sung in his most plaintive voice, this portrayal
of a washed-up bluesman was one of the most
moving moments on the album. Tom Bray
plays the trumpet with Steve Lawrence adding
the atmospheric tenor saxophone. In the song
Young laments all that has been lost so cheap-
ly: "I had a few cheap thrills/But they cost me
a lot more/Than I could give". According to
Young, the song was written late one night in a
hotel room, while on the road. As he recalled:
"I'd been working really hard for a number of
weeks and I was very tired. I hadn't been
sleeping that well. And I was up early and writing the song. And breakfast came. I started
eating and then I started feeling dizzy and really sick. And I thought to myself, 'I'm hitting the
wall... I can't take it anymore; I've pushed
myself so hard, I should go home'. Then I went

back to bed and started to go to sleep. And then I realised that's it. I hit the wall, that's what it was. And I was right back up and finishing the song. It was over before I remembered that I had gotten dizzy and felt sick. So I went back to sleep. That's how those things happen. There's no method."

LIFE IN THE CITY

The powerful brass section is allowed to let rip on this aggressive, urban tale of woe. Young points the finger at property speculators and visualises "Families living under the freeways/It's the American way/Starvin' in the city/While the farm goes to seed/murder in the home and crimes on the street". His acerbic delivery and social conscience pre-empt the epic 'Crime In The City (Sixty To Zero Part 1)' from his next album.

TWILIGHT

Young sets the scene with a beautiful guitar opening, reinforced by trumpet and saxophone. As he noted: "The real difference is I dropped my pick, and started only playing with fingers – and that's much more expressive." A metronome ticks away in the background as the narrator dreams of "Making love to you while time stands still". Twilight is falling, the sun is setting and Young captures the moment, fusing his distinctive guitar work with some fine brass in a poignant arrangement.

MARRIED MAN

This song gets the full Blues Brothers-style brass treatment as Young relates the tale of a married man desperately attempting to maintain his virtue while a temptress hovers nearby. There's an amusingly sanctimonious tone to the lyrics, as Young pleads: "I'm a married man/Respect my happy home.../I work out all day/Take my money back home". Mid-way through the song he manages to sneak in a strong lead break while the brass section blasts out the rhythm.

SUNNY INSIDE

Originally attempted with Crazy Horse back in 1982, this was the oldest composition on the album. The lyrics are nothing more than a simple celebration of life, but their limitations are disguised by the sheer exuberance of the song in which Young pays obvious tribute to the Stax sound.

CAN'T BELIEVE YOUR LYIN'

Young plays a neat blues riff, backed by John Fumo's trumpet and Chad Cromwell's brush strokes on one of the best songs on this album. It turned out to be one of the easiest tracks to complete as Young explained: "I wrote 'Can't Believe Your Lyin'' in five seconds or something. It happened so fast it was like, 'Wow!' We tried it a few different ways with the guys and got it the next day on the second take." The song's story line is familiar B-movie stuff: a man falls for a woman, becomes infatuated, then loses his job, money and friends. Throughout, the chorus portrays the narrator's ambivalence in its ironic lingering refrain: "You have changed my life in so many ways."

HEY HEY

Another barnstorming brass workout for the Blue Notes as Young fastidiously outlines the type of woman he prefers. In playing the sexist blues brother, Young clearly relishes what is as much a thespian as a musical challenge. As he explained: "It's not so much the song as it is the personality of the singer... There's an identity that comes to me, and it's deep. That content of the songs and the attitude of the singing all comes to me at once." Mid-way through the song he gets in another dig at MTV, demanding that couch potatoes get up and dance.

ONE THING

Drummer Ralph Molina and former Rockets' bassist George Whitsall make guest appearances on the album's closing track. Young's playing and singing are sensitively handled here as he relates the sad story of a relationship heading inexorably for the rocks. So ends the most successful of Young's genre experiments during the Eighties.

AMERICAN DREAM

ORIGINAL RELEASE DATE: NOVEMBER 1988

It was widely publicised that, in the event of Crosby overcoming his heroin addiction, Young would record another CSN&Y album. Initially, there were problems with Geffen Records concerning contractual releases, but once Young moved back to Reprise the reunion was unstoppable. What next emerged was a mirror image of events in 1974. Back then, the quartet had undertaken a massive stadium tour but, frustratingly, failed to complete a studio album. This time around there would be an album, but no attendant tour. Recording began as early as April 1987 with Nash's 'Shadowland', but the bulk of the album was completed in the spring and autumn of the following year.

Ultimately, the work received a mixed reception and the lack of a tour ensured that it was not widely promoted, despite its early chart success. Almost inevitably, Young's contributions were assumed to be the most interesting, but this was not the case. The selections discussed below were reasonably impressive but, taken as a whole, did not reveal Young at his very best. What the album lacked from Young was a contribution to match the grandeur of 'Country Girl', the passion of 'Ohio', the ingenuity of 'Everybody I Love You' or the mystery of 'Pushed It Over The End'. CS&N urgently needed Young's passion and grit in order to produce the record of a lifetime. Instead, they received his softer side. It was as if he'd forgotten about the electric power he had brought to 'Almost Cut My Hair' and now regarded CS&N as the vehicle for his cosier, predominantly harmonic work. Overall, the album was still strong and at nearly an hour in length provided enough opportunity for the participants to show off their talents. It was actually far better than many of us anticipated and showcased the enduring viability of CSN&Y as a creative unit. What was missing was Young at his sharpest, a view that would be doubly underlined when we heard his next solo album.

AMERICAN DREAM

The title track of the album seemed to be inspired by the fall of Jerry Lee Lewis' cousin, the celebrated evangelist Jimmy Swaggart. Young's narrative is a wry look at the private and public reaction to the scandal. In determining where "things went wrong", Young points the finger at the American Dream itself. Hypocrisy and hubris go hand in hand here and the protagonist seems both a subject of fun and sympathy. Musically, the track was most notable for its engaging melody, synthed pipes and glorious CS&N harmonies at key moments in the song. Indeed, when issued as a single, this brought them a minor hit in the UK.

NAME OF LOVE

Here Young uncharacteristically offers a message to world rulers: "Do it in the name of love". In keeping with the CS&N ethos he warns against the dangers of missiles, a somewhat contradictory view considering his previous pro-nuclear statements earlier in the decade. Then again, Young has never been renowned for his consistency of viewpoint. Musically, there's a chance to hear Stills and Young trading solos here, though not to any spectacular effect. In fact the real hero here is Joe Vitale whose exceptional drumming gives the song its edge.

THIS OLD HOUSE

CS&N provide the high harmonies while Young controls the music, assisted by synth programmer Bruce Bell. Lyrically, the song deals with the power of the banks in repossessing property. Young sentimentalises the issues with a House On The Prairie lyric in which kids play on swings, mother tends the garden and the parents plan a kitchen on the spot where they first made love. As far as CSN&Y are concerned it's the musical context that's the problem. The superstar foursome are ill suited to a straight country arrangement of this nature. This song would have been appropriate for 'Old Ways' and is better served by the International Harvesters. At least some critics made an amusing connection by linking the composition with Nash's 'Our House' for which it is, intentionally or otherwise, a witty response.

DRIVIN' THUNDER

Although credited to Stills & Young, it's difficult to imagine what the latter contributed, lyrically or musically. Stills takes the lead vocal, with Young detectable in the chorus. The song is nothing special – more a vehicle for Stills to enjoy a spiky lead guitar break.

FEEL YOUR LOVE

Another predominantly solo effort from Young, with musical assistance from Joe Vitale. Although slight, it's a pretty melody and typical of the type of material that Young appears to associate with CS&N.

NIGHT SONG

The final track on the album is this brooding piece written by Stills and Young. Stills' lead vocal is impressive, while Young provides a passionate and gritty edge to the chorus. What proves most memorable is the intense, interweaving lead guitar work from the two which outclasses anything on the Stills/Young album and reminds us of how important their partnership was at its peak.

Full track listing: American Dream; Got It Made; Name Of Love; Don't Say Goodbye; This Old House; Nighttime For The Generals; Shadowland; Drivin' Thunder; Clear Blue Skies; That Girl; Compass; Soldiers Of Peace; Feel Your Love; Night Song.

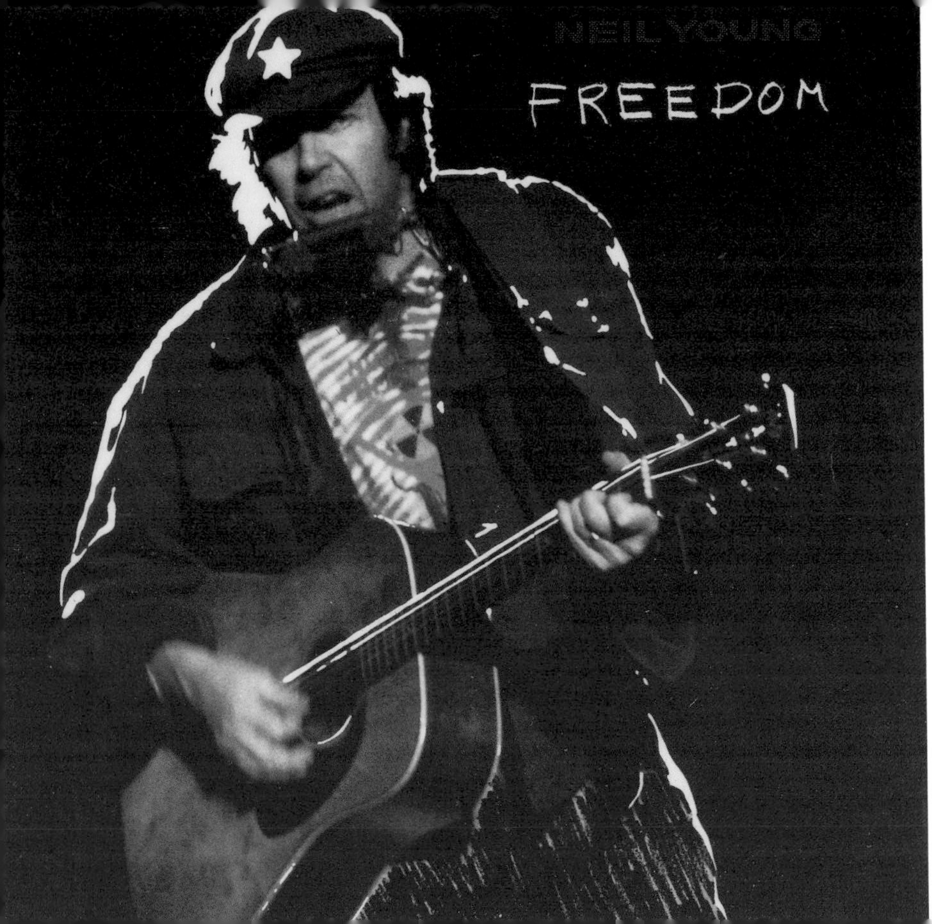
NEIL YOUNG
FREEDOM

FREEDOM

ORIGINAL RELEASE DATE: OCTOBER 1989

In 1989 Young completed work on his next album, tentatively titled 'Times Square', but he was not entirely satisfied with results. By April, he had decided to re-sequence the work and released five of its tracks on the mini-album 'Eldorado', which was only available in Australasia and Japan, where he was touring that same month. The work included 'Don't Cry', 'On Broadway', 'Eldorado', plus two songs unavailable elsewhere. 'Cocaine Eyes' and 'Heavy Love' were roughly hewn, high-powered rock numbers, characterised by snarling guitar work, upfront drumming and rumbling feedback.

Young was determined to improve upon 'Times Square' by producing a work that would finally re-establish his critical reputation at a level last reached with 'Rust Never Sleeps'. The resulting 'Freedom' was a brilliant exercise in playing to his own strengths. It took six of the nine songs from 'Times Square' then added another six. The final album clocked in at an astonishing 61 minutes, more than two-and-a-half times the length of 'Everybody's Rockin'' and with no noticeable fillers. It was easily Young's best album of the decade and an obvious candidate for one of his finest ever. Against the odds, he had ended the decade on the highest point imaginable and his work hereafter would be greeted with seemingly uncritical acceptance.

ROCKIN' IN THE FREE WORLD

Recorded live at Jones Beach, Long Island, this acoustic opener confirmed Young's recent artistic rehabilitation. The title may have sounded like a Status Quo outtake, but such simple sloganeering appealed to Young. As he explained: "I wrote that song out on the road... on my bus, and I thought of the first line and said, 'My God, that really says something but it's such a cliché, it's such an obvious thing', so then I had to use it!"

Judging from the lyrics it seems as though Young has just been on a walkabout of the city's less salubrious areas. He compares himself with Satan in relation to the poor that he encounters on the streets and rails against the deprivation of children whose lives are already blighted by the drug abuse around them. As Young explained to Nick Kent: "The lyrics to 'Rockin' In The Free World' are just a description of events going on every day in America. Sure, I'm concerned for my children, particularly my eldest son... He has to face drugs every day in the school yard, drugs that are way stronger than anything I got offered in most of my years as a professional musician."

CRIME IN THE CITY (SIXTY TO ZERO PART 1)

Young's Dylan-inspired epic, originally 11 verses in concert, is condensed here to a more manageable six stanzas, but still sounds like one of his most impressive songs for years. The opening verse details a bank heist that is transformed into a soap opera by the presence of television cameras. The scene then abruptly shifts to a recording studio where an imperious producer is assembling a backing track at which point he sends for a "hungry songwriter" and in the same breath orders a hamburger. As this section closes, Steve Lawrence's tenor saxophone solo is

the perfect interlude before we're back on the streets and witnessing the problems of a disillusioned cop. Worn down by inept superiors and intimidated by street punks, he feels left with no choice but to "play by their rules". His corruption is frighteningly summed up when he accepts bribes from a 10-year-old kid. During the fourth verse, Young enters more personal territory. The tale of a boy coming to terms with the break-up of his parents' marriage recalls Young's own troubled childhood. By the last verse, Young presents a symbolic précis of his own life beginning with the contention "I keep getting younger" but ending on a more wistful note with the words "wish I never got old".

DON'T CRY

Although just three players appear on this track Young still manages to create havoc with his wall-shattering grunge. He chopped 35 seconds of guitar from the original take on *Eldorado* , explaining that "it wouldn't have got changed if it hadn't been out there". Lyrically the song is 'Don't Cry No Tears' for the grunge age, a more abrasive and insightful look at the anger and guilt surrounding a broken relationship. Vocally, the influence is a surprising one: "That's me totally under the Roy Orbison spell. When I wrote it and recorded it I was thinking, 'Roy Orbison meets thrash metal'." Appropriately, the track closes with a battle royal between Young and drummer Chad Cromwell. The feedback-drenched fade-out features Young's voice calling out in the distance.

HANGIN' ON A LIMB

A remarkable switch of mood as Young reverts to acoustic with Linda Ronstadt providing the backing vocals. It's an upbeat celebration of love rekindled, using the album's title to express the "freedom he thought he didn't know". Like the rest of the work, the song is perfectly produced with Young's acoustic guitar and vocal prominent.

ELDORADO

This morality tale of money and greed south of the border is another of the album's high points. Spanish-influenced guitar and maracas set the scene as Young presents a Western tale, not dissimilar to a Serge Leone film. There's a shoot out, a card game, diamond-clad women and impoverished locals. Mid-way through the narrative, Young switches to a contemporary setting as an unnamed individual closes a deal, boards a plane and snaps his briefcase shut. It could be a drug deal or a political pay-off but the feeling conveyed is of a country bought and sold. Throughout, Young's precise, expressive guitar playing adds a poignant air which continues through the final verse which presents a bull fight as everyday ritual. Young is at his most passionate here, screaming the vocal as an explosive guitar brings the song to a dramatic peak.

THE WAYS OF LOVE

Vintage Young inasmuch as it was written during the mid-Seventies. This could easily have slotted into 'Comes A Time', with its simple expression of the wins and losses of love, complemented by Ben Keith's steel guitar and Linda Ronstadt's harmony. The song is superior among its kind and a conscious attempt by Young to bridge his new work with his old. As he admitted: "I did a session of older songs, some of them 15 years old, just songs that I had around. And I got two of those, 'Ways Of Love' and 'Too Far Gone' that I thought were good... and so I had a base for something... people could hear these songs on *Freedom* and relate them to whatever it is they liked about me 15 years ago... it reaches back, like a root."

SOMEDAY

Sampedro excels on keyboards here as Young weaves another enticing tune which includes some wry remarks about television preachers, recalling the theme of 'American Dream'. The backing vocals are also amusing, imitating the sound of aeroplanes and industrial workers in different verses. The songs end in a clash of brass and steel which is most effective.

ON BROADWAY

Reviving The Drifters' 1963 hit might not seem the best idea on an all new album such as this, but as a cover it works reasonably well. The electric treatment takes the composition into Young's sphere and he attempts to make the song his own with the words "But they're dead wrong/I know they are/Cause I can play this here guitar", upon which he bursts into a feedback frenzy. In keeping with 'Rockin' In The

Free World' and 'Crime In The City', he turns his attention to drug dealing on the streets ending the song with the urgent cry "Give me some of that crack/Give me that crack".

WRECKING BALL

An engaging piano opening sets the scene for what seems a slice of autobiography: "My life's an open book/You read it on the radio". The narrative then moves into the past with romantic visions of the wrecking ball and a date dressed in virgin white. Young even throws in an allusion from 'Like A Hurricane' ("Shining from star to star"). It's an enticing lilt with an air of adolescent insecurity neatly captured in the lines, "But I won't telephone/ 'Cause you might say hello/What is it that makes me feel this way?"

NO MORE

Young reverts to his Crazy Horse style of guitar playing for this minor classic. The first verse alludes to drug addiction with the narrator admitting "'Cause not so long ago/It had a hold on me/I couldn't let it go". The overall feel of the song is distinctly elegiac, giving the impression that something intangible has been lost. In the final verse, the corrupted quest could be referring to drugs, music, or both: "Searchin' for quality/Havin' to have the very best/Now scrounging' for quantity..." Young prefers to retain the sense of mystery and ambiguity that is central to the song's theme. As he duly pointed out to the *Village Voice*'s Jimmy McDonough: "If you listen to the lyrics – really listen to the lyrics – I'm not saying anything definitely. It's completely ambiguous what's going on, and that's the feeling of 'No More'. How many times do you have to say 'no more' before it means 'no more'? Because that song doesn't mean 'no more'." When issued as a CD promo, this track included an additional live version taped from *Saturday Night Live*.

TOO FAR GONE

This again harked back to the Seventies when Young was going through his "bar culture"

phase. It's a dark romantic song with acoustic guitar and mandolin accompaniment. Simple though the lyrics are, Young still manages to throw in a memorable couplet: "We had drugs and we had booze/But we still had plenty to lose".

ROCKIN' IN THE FREE WORLD

In common with 'Rust Never Sleeps', the album ends with an electric version of its opening acoustic number. The effect is to create a staggeringly powerful conclusion in which Young's passionate urgency drives him on relentlessly. He slips in an extra verse towards the end with the political barb: "We got a kinder, gentler machine-gun hand". The refrain, simple yet effective, ends the album on a suitably high note. By then you realise that you have witnessed Young's most eclectic and accomplished album of the decade.

RAGGED GLORY

ORIGINAL RELEASE DATE: SEPTEMBER 1990

In the wake of 'Freedom', critics were falling over themselves to praise Young's work. He could hardly have planned a more opportune moment to reunite with Crazy Horse who had been in exile since the tetchy 1987 tour. Unlike the patchy 'Life', 'Ragged Glory' revealed Crazy Horse at their most raucous, playing the no-holds barred rock that made them such favourites to a generation of Young fans. With their grunge-style now the height of fashion, the album was perfectly timed. It was the classic example of raw excitement overcoming substance. Critical hyperbole conveniently ignored the fact that the songs weren't that strong by Young's best standards, while the extended guitar forays failed to match the power and passion of Crazy Horse's finest work. The album lacked both the depth of 'Everybody Knows This Is Nowhere' and the passion of 'Tonight's The Night' but offered a spontaneity which produced a fairly good imitation of vintage Crazy Horse and allowed Young to play to the gallery as an ageing guitar god.

COUNTRY HOME

Formerly known as 'Spud Blues', this country-influenced composition dated back to the Seventies. Although not one of Young's greatest compositions it provided a reasonable workout for Crazy Horse. The chiming guitar work is arresting throughout, but the ending is overdone by a blast of feedback which stretches the song to seven-and-a-half minutes in length.

WHITE LINE

Originally featured on the unreleased album 'Homegrown', this was another song from two decades ago that Young dusted off for the Crazy Horse reunion. Again, it's a good song but no classic and you have to wonder why Young felt the sudden need to search the vaults for relatively average material.

F*!#IN' UP

Crude, both in its obscene title and execution, this was nevertheless a concert favourite. Young clearly enjoyed playing the simple, but insistent, riff which was perfect for Crazy Horse. As Young modestly noted: "We knew we weren't any good. We knew none of us could really play. We'd get it in the first take every time and it was never right – but we would never do it any better. We're making mistakes, but what happens is we get so into the music it sounds great."

OVER AND OVER

Young's vocal gets decidedly tuneless here, but he manages to find a half-decent riff and some mildly evocative and amusing lyrics ("Somewhere in the fire of love our dreams went up in smoke"). The piece ends in 30 seconds of feedback, for no apparent reason beyond annoying radio programmers. According to Young, the group had some teething troubles with this track: "I remember when I did that I called up Frank Sampedro and I was trying to play it... The first time we were learning it we could never get it together. So I called him up and left a message on his answering service and I went, 'OK, Frank, this is it. It's like one, two, three, doo, doo, do...'. All that time we had trouble getting it, it was the count. When I gave him the count, he could just listen to the tape over and over again where it started on a four instead of a one. Ever since then we've locked in."

LOVE TO BURN

At over 10 minutes in length, this was one of the key moments on the album. It's stronger than the preceding material with Young and Crazy Horse finding a groove in which to jam persuasively. It may not be 'Cowgirl In The Sand', but it has its moments. Lyrically, it deals with life's tribulations, including the break-up of a family, a theme which Young acknowledged was "painfully personal". As he concluded: "In the song you got all these things happening and you've just got to go for it. Just got to keep trying to give, keep trying to stay open. You can't shut down because of all the bad stories, the bad news movies that happen in life."

FARMER JOHN

Completed on the last day of recording for the

album, this was a throwaway but playful look back to Young's garage group youth. Written by Don And Dewey in 1959, it became a US Top 20 hit for The Premiers five years later and was frequently played by The Squires. Its mindless drone suited this most basic of albums. As Young wryly observed: "'Farmer John' was good for those college bars in the East. I see Daisy Mae from *Li'l Abner* every time I hear that song."

MANSION ON THE HILL

One of the highlights of the album was this composition, often assumed to have been inspired by Charles Manson. The couplet "There's a mansion on the hill/Psychedelic music fills the air" places the song firmly in the Sixties with Young looking back to that era for cold comfort. Young recalls an amusing moment during the recording when they needlessly ran through various versions of the song: "We were trying to get the groove on 'Mansion On The Hill' but we didn't know we'd recorded it a week-and-a-half earlier. We forgot about the one on record because we never listen to playbacks. We were working trying to get the song right and we'd already done it

and didn't know!" The CD single of 'Mansion On The Hill' featured the otherwise unavailable grunge celebration 'Don't Spook The Horse'.

DAYS THAT USED TO BE

Written on Young's boat *WN Ragland* in 1988, this emerged at a time when he seemed steeped in the influence of mid-period Bob Dylan. The entire tune sounds like a remake of 'My Back Pages' and there's even a guitar break smack in the middle that recalls McGuinn's solo on The Byrds' version of the song. Young reluctantly admitted the profound Dylan connection: "It is the same melody in three or four notes, and there's no doubt about that, but it lends itself to bringing you back there... it's in keeping with what the song is about to have a nostalgic twist in it." Indeed, as Young concludes: "There's very few of us left from the days that used to be".

LOVE AND ONLY LOVE

This second 10-minute extravaganza features a Jimi Hendrix-like opening which brilliantly sets the mood. Although it fails to equal the best of Young's collaborations with Crazy Horse it features all the ingredients that make the partnership work. Ultimately, it's those Hendrix flourishes that elevate the song above the ordinary and Young even throws in a few portentous lyrics ("Love and only love will endure") like a minor Biblical prophet. The recording was a matter of selecting which version of the song was best. As Young explained: "There are three different takes of 'Love And Only Love'. Each one is completely different. Two are over 10 minutes, the other is over nine. One's really fast, another really slow. The slow one is angelic – the upside of the song. The fast one is pretty much the upside of it too. But the middle one – the one we used – there's really a battle going on. A battle between good and bad... We actually overdubbed 'Love And Only Love' three times. It was all so much fun, the work didn't seem to matter."

MOTHER EARTH (NATURAL ANTHEM)

Recorded at the Hoosier Dome Farm Aid benefit in Indianapolis, with some vocals added back in Redwood, this was an extremely effective album closer, fusing feedback and choral into a hymn to Mother Nature. The simple sentiment "Respect Mother Earth and her healing ways/Or trade away our children's days" reflected Young's increasing interest in ecology. He spoke in a surprisingly forthright way about the issues: "Peace and love, the environment, Mother Nature – that's going to come in the Nineties because the children of the Eighties picked up on all the things that were going on and they are still wide open and see the truth in it."

ARC/WELD

ORIGINAL RELEASE DATE: OCTOBER 1991

On paper, this album seemed less than riveting. Straight after 'Ragged Glory', Young provides us with a live double of recent favourites and the package features only one unreleased song: a striking version of Dylan's 'Blowin' In The Wind'. Not only that but no less than six of the songs had already received a live airing on Young's 'Live Rust'. For those who recalled the extraordinary live versions of 'Ordinary People' and 'Sixty To Zero', it was difficult to avoid the initial conclusion that Young had chosen the wrong tour to document. For a man with a wealth of unissued live material, it was frustrating to consider that he was again releasing such familiar songs.

Fortunately, such negative reasoning could be easily forgotten amid the thrill of hearing over two hours of Young at his searing best. Here was a live album that truly captured the verve and excitement of a performer reaching new peaks. Much of the intensity came from playing concerts while the Gulf War raged. As Young noted: "It blew my head off during that tour. When we were playing that stuff, it was intense. It was real. I could see people dying in my mind. I could see bombs falling, buildings collapsing on families." *Weld* proved a memorable souvenir of the Smell The Horse tour, with several of the songs from his last album sounding even better in a concert setting. The critical response to this album was universally positive and for those intrigued by Young's love of sonic experimentation there was the optional bonus of the 35-minute 'Arc', in which he transformed feedback, vocal fragments and distorted endings into a sound collage.

Full track listing: Hey Hey, My My (Into The Black); Crime In The City; Blowin' In The Wind; Welfare Mothers; Love To Burn; Cinnamon Girl; Mansion On The Hill; F*!#in' Up; Cortez The Killer; Powderfinger; Love And Only Love; Rockin' In The Free World; Like A Hurricane; Farmer John; Tonight's The Night; Roll Another Number. Arc.

HARVEST MOON

ORIGINAL RELEASE DATE: NOVEMBER 1992

Widely touted as the belated follow-up to 'Harvest', this was a significantly different record from its 1972 semi-electric counterpart. An all-acoustic affair, it was far more reflective and laid-back, indicating Young's musings on family life and encroaching middle age. Once again, its timing was apt. It almost seemed as though Young was deliberately showing off his acoustic credentials in order to heighten the contrast with the electric 'Ragged Glory'. The truth was that he needed to tone down the volume of his music as much for medical as aesthetic reasons. With his hearing impaired by the deafening tour with Crazy Horse, the mellow tones of 'Harvest Moon' were an obvious panacea. At times the record was almost soporific. The tunes were simple, appealing and well crafted but devoid of passion or musical eccentricity. For once, the sum of the album was somehow lesser than its parts. But it was a pleasant enough record on its own terms even if it sounded less interesting than his previous pastoral albums. What it offered was Young coming to terms with his past in a quietly sentimental and nostalgic mood. As he explained: "I think the album's saying that it's OK that some things don't last forever. It doesn't mean you have to stop living or loving or experiencing things."

UNKNOWN LEGEND

This attractive opening track is highly reminiscent of Young's work on 'Comes A Time'. Indeed, the song was written only a few years after that album was released. Here, he presents an idealised portrayal of a woman, who nevertheless was earthy enough to work in a diner and ride a Harley Davidson. The character sounds like a composite of his current and ex-wife, and as Young adds: "It's inspired by some people I know and some people I don't know and all kinds of things put together... They're just pictures, people's lives. A lot of the common thing is survival, not losing what it is you were when you were young, but take it with you, take it with you into your own age, don't leave it behind."

FROM HANK TO HENDRIX

Although the tone is quieter, this is the old *Harvest* team of The Stray Gators with familiar guests James Taylor and Linda Ronstadt. Like much of the album, the song reflects on passing time, catalogued by different cult heroes from Hank Marvin to Jimi Hendrix, Marilyn Monroe to Madonna. There's also the threat of a long-term relationship heading for the divorce courts. "Well that's part of the story," Young noted. "There's a whole bunch of things in there... You're constantly wondering which way things are going to go. Whether it's going to last or whether it's going to explode. That's part of the romantic relationship, certain amounts of turmoil." Although the narrator is self-questioning, the predominant mood is stoical, with Young concluding: "The same thing that makes you live/Can kill you in the end".

YOU AND ME

This was the first song written for the album and part of it dates back as far as 1971. When he appeared at the LA Music Center on 1 February of that year, Young began 'I Am A Child' with the words: "I was thinking of you and me/Making love beneath the tree/And now I

wonder, could it be?" At the time, many of us thought this was part of the song, but it was obviously a fragment begun at that time and left unfinished for 20 years.

As Young joked: "I always liked the beginning of it, now it's nice to hear the end!" It's a charming composition which even manages an allusion to 'Old Man' with Young now casting himself in the older role.

HARVEST MOON

Opening with the sound of a broom sweeping, this pleasing melody recalls The Everly Brothers' 'Walk Right Back'. Lyrically, it's a simple enough nostalgic piece, re-enacting the heroine's dance beneath the harvest moon. Young wallows in the sentimentality but also expresses the need to reaffirm old vows.

WAR OF MAN

Inspired by the Gulf War, this ecology song followed Young's comments on the plight of helpless animals caught up in the conflict. The arrangement is not particularly exciting but the fifth verse introduces Linda Ronstadt, Nicolette Larson and Young's step-sister Astrid singing lead together which is very effective.

ONE OF THESE DAYS

Arguably one of the best songs on the album, this is a wistful and endearing tribute to all the friends and collaborators who contributed to Young's life and career, from the country fiddler to the rock'n'roll players. In writing his fantasy letter, Young provides a neat summation of his career "From down in LA/All the way to Nashville/New York City/To my Canadian prairie home/My friends are scattered/Like leaves from an old maple".

SUCH A WOMAN

Arranged by Jack Nitzsche and recorded at Sunset Sound, this slight composition strains under the weight of an 18-piece string section. The melody isn't particularly striking but the performance is strong and the lyrics neatly bypass the saccharine by stressing a relationship in terms of shared pain as well as love. The song subsequently appeared on single in 1994, backing 'Philadelphia', a Young song otherwise available only on film soundtrack.

OLD KING

The only genuinely exuberant moment on the album comes with this hilarious tribute to Young's tick hound Elvis. In order to avoid misinterpretation, the dog's name is changed to King for the purpose of the song. The composition is a welcome moment of lightness amid the lugubrious reflections on life, which is doubly ironic when you consider that the subject matter is the dog's death. Young's approach is thankfully unsentimental: "Old King meant a lot to me/But that hound dog is history". The banjo carries the tune well and overall the track deserves to be placed among the great canine songs of country rock like 'Old Blue'.

DREAMIN' MAN

This features one of Young's best vocals on the album and the playing, though understated, is also impressive. Ostensibly, the lyrics appear to be a simple reiteration of "I am just a dreamer" from 'Like A Hurricane', but there's an underlying sinister aspect as the narrator reveals himself as a gun-toting stalker. Weirdly, neither the vocals nor the music convey any sense of this drama and it's only the closing refrain ("He's got a problem") that makes you realise that you haven't misread the lyric sheet.

NATURAL BEAUTY

This 10-minute closing track was recorded live at the Civic Auditorium, Portland. It's a some-times intriguing song with Young taking on the nature/artifice dichotomy like a sixteenth-century poet. The key lines "A natural beauty should be/Preserved like a monument to nature" are paradoxical, for beauty like nature itself is mutable. The song closes with the sound of a harmonica, before leading into 'Dawn Chorus', excerpted from the album 'A Month In The Brazilian Rainforest'. As Young insisted: "The environment is really important to me... at least for me to do my part... to keep the ball rolling for the planet. I think organisations like 'Earth First' have a reason to be there. Even though vigilanteism *per se* may not be something I'd be 100 per cent behind, in this particular case what we are talking about is the Earth being raped and governments not coming to its defence. Even being on the opposite side of the fence on many times, I consider myself a citizen of planet Earth first and a citizen of whatever country second."

LUCKY THIRTEEN

ORIGINAL RELEASE DATE: JANUARY 1993

Reputedly compiled by Young , this intriguing compilation attempted to make some sense of the Geffen years. Essentially, it's an exercise in eclecticism, pulling the better moments from generally weak albums and making you feel that several were rather better than you remember. The two best songs from 'Trans' are included, with 'Sample And Hold' featured in an extended eight-minute version. Although the choices from 'Old Ways' are more contentious, it was probable that a song like 'Misfits' was regarded as less representative of that album's pastoral spirit. Thankfully, Young tastefully plucks 'Hippie Dream' and 'Mideast Vacation' (two of his better songs of the era from less impressive works) and ends the compilation with a stirring live version of the audience favourite 'This Note's For You'. There were also four songs previously unreleased in any form:

DEPRESSION BLUES

Once intended for the cancelled Farm Aid EP, this song was part of the original unissued 'Old Ways'. It's an impressive track with harmonica, fiddle and steel guitar prominent. Set in the Depression years, it portrays a world of property speculators and ordinary people relieving their problems by visiting movie houses for entertainment. Young has claimed that the original 'Old Ways' recalled the commercial side of 'Harvest', but this track confirms that it was surely a lot closer to the traditional Nashville spirit of the later 'Old Ways'. It's easy to see why Geffen might have been cautious about marketing this despite its undoubted quality.

GET GONE

Recorded with The Shocking Pinks at Hara Arena, Dayton, Ohio, this is another extremely derivative rock'n'roll number with a melody recalling 'Willie And The Hand Jive', 'Mona' and 'Not Fade Away'. It's still better than much of 'Everybody's Rockin'' though and serves as an amusing biography of Young's imaginary Fifties' group.

DON'T TAKE YOUR LOVE AWAY FROM ME

Also recorded live at the Hara Arena, this song showed how much better The Shocking Pinks' experiment sounded live. At over six minutes in length this song is the equivalent of 25 per cent

of the entire 'Everybody's Rockin''. It is almost as if Young was attempting to compensate for that parsimonious offering by presenting some new songs to expunge the memory of its lesser moments. If only this track had featured on the album, it might have tempered some of the critical outcries.

AIN'T IT THE TRUTH

Although embarrassingly insubstantial as a song, this Blue Notes' live recording had some historical value as it was one of Young's earliest compositions and part of The Squires' early Sixties' repertoire. It's stretched out to a ludicrous seven-and-a-half minutes with its basic riff and banal lyrics blown out of all proportion by the brass section. Along the way Young offers some dietary advice: "Eat watermelon/Eat peaches and cream/Eat ripe tomatoes".

Full track listing: Sample And Hold; Transformer Man; Depression Blues; Get Gone; Don't Take Your Love Away From Me; Once An Angel; Where Is The Highway Tonight?; Hippie Dream; Pressure; Around The World; Mideast Vacation; Ain't It The Truth; This Note's For You.

UNPLUGGED

ORIGINAL RELEASE DATE: JUNE 1993

MTV's *Unplugged* series offered artistes the opportunity to present their electric material in an acoustic setting. The news that Young was to be featured was eagerly anticipated as he was widely respected as one of the most eclectic and inventive performers in rock music. The resultant album, although a reasonable distillation of his career, proved only partially successful. Some songs were performed solo, while others included his band, featuring Nils Lofgren, Ben Keith, Spooner Oldham, Tim Drummond, Oscar Butterworth and backing singers Nicolette Larson and Astrid Young. The highlight of the evening was the one new song that Young introduced: 'Stringman'. Dating back to 1976, this impressive ballad was allegedly inspired by Stephen Stills, a view which, if true, pays enormous tribute to its subject ("There is no dearer friend of mine that I know in this life"). If only Young had featured a couple more unissued songs of this quality then the album would have been a major event. Unfortunately, it was weakened by songs already familiar in an acoustic setting, most notably the three selections from the recent 'Harvest Moon', which sounded like Young taking the easy option. There were, however, some welcome surprises: an acoustic 'Mr Soul' that gave the song a fresh, moodier edge; a fascinating 'Transformer Man' which, minus the vocoders, took on a greater poignancy; and, most intriguingly, 'Like A Hurricane' played on a pump organ. The last three were radical enough to show what Young might have done throughout the evening had he been in a more inventive frame of mind.

Full track listing of album: The Old Laughing Lady; Mr Soul; World On A String; Pocahontas; Stringman; Like A Hurricane; The Needle And The Damage Done; Helpless; Harvest Moon; Transformer Man; Unknown Legend; Look Out For My Love; Long May You Run; From Hank To Hendrix.

sleeps
with angels
happen
too late too soon
too late too soon
neil young and crazy horse

SLEEPS WITH ANGELS

ORIGINAL RELEASE DATE: SEPTEMBER 1994

Having impressed critics with successive electric and acoustic studio albums that essentially recalled former glories, Young urgently needed to present his public with something challenging and new. He intended to record an album with Booker T and the MGs, with whom he had toured in 1993. However, that idea was abandoned when MG's bassist Donald "Duck" Dunn revealed that he had cancer of the throat. Soon, Young was back with Crazy Horse but then further bad news affected his creative progress when he learned that Nirvana's Kurt Cobain had taken his life. Worse still, his suicide note had quoted lines from Young's 'My My, Hey Hey (Into The Blue)': "It's better to burn out than to fade away". Young was shocked into composing a new album whose sombre mood and general air of mystery recalled his greatest work of the mid-Seventies. The fact that he refused to undertake any promotion or explain the lyrics behind the songs made the album seem even more intriguing. Here Young was moving away from the recent clever pastiches of his old material to produce a genuinely riveting work that was strange, unclassifiable and among the best of his albums. It was heartening to know that after nearly 30 years Young still had the capacity to disturb and intrigue.

MY HEART

Proof that Young is back on the move creatively is provided during the opening minutes of the album. Suddenly, fresh instruments are introduced to the Crazy Horse repertoire which provide a new dimension to the music. Frank Sampedro adds an ethnic flavour to the proceedings with a marimba, a South American instrument originating in Guatemala which contributes a buzzing effect to the lower notes. Young meanwhile plays a "tack piano", which sounds as though it has been on loan to a saloon bar in a Western. The effect is to dislodge the song from contemporary rock into another age. Meanwhile, Young's vocal is pitched high like a child's while Crazy Horse add a hymnal backing which is decidedly eerie. It's a fascinating opening to what will prove one of Young' most unusual and startling albums.

PRIME OF LIFE

Crazy Horse's backing vocals are again called upon here to enhance the mood. The oblique lyrics picture a king, a queen and "a roomful of paper dolls" with a growling lead guitar in the background that sounds like it is straining to be unleashed. But what disorientates the listener is the flute backing. Young is no woodwind player and the so-called "flute" in the credits sounds more like a tin whistle. Stranger still, it's completely out of tune to the point where it's almost painful to listen to. It must be one of the worst performances of the instrument ever committed to a professional recording. Despite that, the song is still intriguing.

DRIVEBY

Like many of the tracks on the album, this has a strangely mesmeric feel while the lyrics simmer with images of violence. The song was apparently inspired by the death of a young girl, shot from a car driving by. Young's vocal is impressive and

the electric and acoustic guitar interplay gives the song an added tension. The rumbling feedback is used sparingly as if to create a sense of tension rather than full-blown mayhem.

SLEEPS WITH ANGELS

The title track is one of the most powerful songs that Young has recorded in recent years. Its theme unfolds gradually moving from the early description of the relationship between the two protagonists to a more rounded portrayal of Courtney Love as a teen queen making things happen and finally desperately phoning friends on the evening of her lover's death. The simple dour chanting of "Too late" and "Too soon" is Crazy Horse's equivalent of a Greek chorus and a curt reminder of the terrible banality of Cobain's suicide.

WESTERN HERO

This thoughtful ballad recalls the theme of Donovan's 'Universal Soldier' using selected moments in history to speculate on violence and war. Young's Western hero is pictured hanging up his six-gun, a redundant figure whose old form of frontier justice is being swept away by social change. The action then leaps forward fifty years to the Second World War and the Invasion of Normandy. Even that recent glory is seen as transient with the battle hero a mere shadow ("But now he's just a memory"). With Young's accordion and Sampedro's grand piano enhancing the melody, the song moves into its final phase, taking us to the present where the hero seems tarnished by avarice ("Here comes a Western hero... big money in his hand"). The nature of warfare has also altered to the point where complete annihilation is a cold consideration ("The bombs burst in the air/This time we're never going back").

CHANGE YOUR MIND

At 14 minutes 39 seconds, this is not only the longest song on the album, but the longest studio song Young has ever released. It is also the most sustained attempt to rekindle the original sound of Crazy Horse with a song whose gradual build-up recalls the structure of 'Cowgirl In The Sand' rather than the single incandescent bursts evident on 'Ragged Glory'. Lyrically, the song is a testament to the empowering nature of love. The first movement expresses the "magic touch" in strictly affirmative terms: "distracting", "supporting",

"embracing" and "convincing". Young's lead guitar breaks are slow and precise, recalling 'Like A Hurricane', but minus the pyrotechnics. The next chorus continues the ascending movement: "protecting", "restoring", "revealing", "soothing". By the third chorus, however, there is a distinct shift in tone as the adjectives reveal the love as destructive as well as beneficial: "destroying", "confining", "distorting", "controlling". Crazy Horse's replies are sung like a mantra. In fact, the hymnal quality of the song is its most distinctive trait, in keeping with the sombre elegy that inspired the work. The erotic imagery and call-and-response conclusion is both very soothing and disturbing.

BLUE EDEN

This song picks up the mantra from 'Change Your Mind' with its opening line repeating: "Embracing, distorting, supporting, comforting". A rough blues, the song has that same jarring tone that 'Vampire Blues' brought to 'On The Beach'. The lyrics, elliptical and inconclusive, add to the listener's sense of unease.

SAFEWAY CART

Talbot's throbbing bass line is at the centre of this disconcerting vision of a "ghetto dawn" filled with vague images filtered through a television screen. While Sampedro adds to the effects with a Wurlitzer piano and Obenheim synth, Young appears on guitar and harmonica. He also attempts some further flute playing, this time barely audible during the closing seconds of the track.

TRAIN OF LOVE

This is 'Western Hero' revisited as Young plays exactly the same tune over a lyric that uses the train as a metaphor for the troubled route of love. In fact, this is a composite of several other songs on the album and serves as a refrain of the central theme. Note how the lyrics of 'Blue Eden' are repeated here like a prayer: "It's part of me and part of you".

TRANS AM

Young's love of trains resurfaces for one of the more lyrical songs on the album. Once again, Young commutes between past and present, delving deep into the Old West for snatched conversations about a massacre.

The speaker recalls riding the Sante Fe before the tracks were laid for the Trans Am. By the third verse, the time scheme shifts to the present where we witness an international sales conference amid an earthquake. The indomitable Trans Am negotiates the tremor by "bouncing around" and finding another road. In the final verse, Young reveals his fascination with train collecting, eagerly detailing the story of two comrades who set out to rescue an abandoned train and restore her to glory. Throughout the song, both Young's guitar solo and vocal are suitably restrained.

PIECE OF CRAP

The joker in the pack, this is Young and Crazy Horse in playful mood. Comic lyrics collide with the affected New York drawl of the chorus, to humorous effect. As a protest against the instant obsolescence of modern-day consumer products, the song reminds the listener of the contrasting reverence Young shows toward classic design: most notably in his love of the aforementioned 'Trans Am'.

A DREAM THAT CAN LAST

The song opens with Young apparently testing

his tack piano which soon reverts to its familiar Last Chance Saloon Bar ambience. It's rather like being abruptly transported back to the Old West but for Young this seems just a stop off on a more cosmological journey: "I feel like I died and went to heaven". The track is chillingly atmospheric with Molina's bass thumping like an amplified heartbeat as Young once more speaks the words of angels. It's a thrilling conclusion to one of Young's best albums.

MIRROR BALL

ORIGINAL RELEASE DATE: JUNE 1995

Young's connection with Pearl Jam dated back to 1993 when they shared the bill with him at a number of dates and sometimes joined him on-stage. There were similar get-togethers later, most notably at Young's Rock'n'Roll Hall of Fame induction dinner in January 1995. Soon after, Young and Pearl Jam convened at Seattle's Bad Animals and hastily completed an album in two sessions, with Brendan O'Brien at the controls. The work brought Young's music to a fresh generation of listeners and satisfied the curiosity of those anxious to learn how he would sound playing with a younger version of Crazy Horse. This cross-generational experiment was nothing less than exciting with Young breaking free of such requisites as rehearsals and tuning sessions to deliver some of his most searing moments. The album's flaws are inextricably linked to its strengths. Spontaneity and passion are there in abundance, but there are more bum notes and unde-veloped songs than usual. Young sounds like he is battling against the clock, as if he believes or realises that the collaboration is a now or never event. That tension provides the album with its distinctive edge while also robbing it of greater glory.

SONG X

The first of two songs directly focusing on the abortion issue sees Young attempting to adopt a neutral stance. His usual harangues against religion, familiar from such songs as 'Love In Mind' and 'Soldier', are more restrained here, although he still manages to portray the sandy-haired priest as an agent of retribution. Musically, the track is a fascinating departure for Young who still sounds fresh and inventive with his new associates Pearl Jam. He manages to produce a veritable grunge sea shanty, reinforced by an electric guitar solo of wall-trembling intensity.

ACT OF LOVE

Although premièred in live performance with

Crazy Horse, this was the track that brought Young and Pearl Jam together. Again, sex and religion are the central themes: Young presents a Holy War in which abortion is the key issue, but also reveals the callousness of a father who avoids parental responsibilities: "I know I said I'd help you baby/Here's my wallet call me some-time". The constant use of the word "baby" directed at the woman unerringly focuses the lis-tener's attention on the likely aborted offspring. In the background, Young and Pearl Jam cross swords in a fierce guitar duel.

I'M THE OCEAN

The most obscure song on the album sees Young writing in a stream of consciousness mode complete with seemingly unconnected couplets. There is also a shifting time scheme, moving from the present to a past in which a chieftain and his braves roam the plains. Jack Irons' drumming is unrelenting, burying Young's piano deep in the middle of a chaotic mix. Lyrically the song ends with a wonderfully hallu-cinogenic self-description: "I'm a drug that makes you dream/I'm an aerostar/I'm a cutlass supreme in the wrong lane..."

BIG GREEN COUNTRY

The narrative is again set in the Old West with painted braves awaiting a kill. A woman waits hopefully, praying for her cowboy hero who is described in terms which suggest Young has been watching the Marlboro cigarette adverts: "Over the hill in the big green country, that's the place where the cancer cowboy rides". The song sounds more ramshackle as it progresses, with Young singing painfully in the upper register with lyrics that sound like the ramblings of a stoned surrealist: "Sometimes I feel like a piece of paper/Sometimes I feel like my own name..."

TRUTH BE KNOWN

Eddie Vedder is prominent on backing vocals as Young plays a basic riff set against a lyric about fading dreams and lost friendships. Young reflects on both in the closing lines, "When the fire that once was your friend burns your fingers to the bone and your song meets a sudden end echoing through right and wrong".

DOWNTOWN

Young utters an obscenity before the song breaks into its simple but irresistible groove. The lyrics are lighter and more amusing than anything else on the album as he imagines hippies traipsing downtown to dance the Charleston and the Limbo. If this suggests a lampoon of senile Sixties' relics then Young is equally quick to pay tribute to his heroes, affectionately picturing Jimi Hendrix playing in the back room while Led Zeppelin are on-stage. Having recently performed alongside Jimmy Page at the Rock'n'Roll Hall of Fame, Young pays him a passing tribute, describing "A note from Page like a water-wasted diamond". As the song ends, Young exclaims with evident satisfaction: "That's funky!" Speaking to the *NME,* he confirmed that the song was inspired by the Hall of Fame appearance: "There was all these crazy people there that I recognised from all different periods of time in rock'n'roll. I guess that's what the song is really about. It's like, they're there. They're all there still singing and playing. It's just a place you can only go to in your mind – downtown, and whoever you like the best is going to be who's playing in the club."

WHAT HAPPENED YESTERDAY
Only 45 seconds and 25 words long, this is the shortest song Young ever released. It's a brief reflection on the past sung in that familiar high vocal that he occasionally uses for anguished effect.

PEACE AND LOVE
One of the more memorable tunes on the album, this continues Young's confused views on hippie values, including a reference to John Lennon's death. Eddie Vedder composes and sings his own riposte to Young, reflecting on the grunge generation's outside view of the flights and follies of rock culture and inability to extract anything more than its superficial rewards: "I saw the dream I saw the wake/We shared it all but not the take".

THROW YOUR HATRED DOWN
Young's plea for peace fuses hippie dreams with grunge aggression in what is actually one of the weaker tracks on the album. The lyrics are extravagant but portentous ("In the underworld the weaknesses are seen by peasants and presidents who plan the counter-scheme"). Occasionally it sounds like automatic writing as Young indicated when he feebly attempted to articulate the song's meaning: "'Throw Your Hatred Down' is kind of hard to describe

visually. It's a physical thing that might have been in my head. I still can see this... but I can't see what it is."

SCENERY

Young is at his most cynical here puncturing the American Dream with sarcastic asides about the "home of the brave" and "land of the free", a place where "when you earn their trust then you are truly in danger".

FALLEN ANGEL

Young's pump organ ends the album with this very short song whose melody is identical to the aforementioned 'I'm The Ocean'.

INDEX